CAKE
Decorating
BASICS

CAKE Decorating BASICS

Techniques and tips for creating
beautiful cakes

RACHEL BROWN

NEW
HOLLAND

Published in 2007 by

New Holland Publishers (UK) Ltd

London • Cape Town • Sydney • Auckland

www.newhollandpublishers.com

Garfield House, 86–88 Edgware Road, London W2 2EA, United Kingdom

80 McKenzie Street, Cape Town 8001, South Africa

14 Aquatic Drive, Frenchs Forest, NSW 2086, Australia

218 Lake Road, Northcote, Auckland, New Zealand

ISBN 978 1 84537 518 8

EDITOR: Anne Konopelski

EDITORIAL DIRECTION: Rosemary Wilkinson

DESIGN: Casebourne Rose Design Associates

PHOTOGRAPHY: Shona Wood

ARTWORK: Carrie Hill and Sue Rose

PRODUCTION: Hazel Kirkman

10 9 8 7 6 5 4 3 2 1

Reproduction by Pica Digital Ltd, Singapore

Printed and bound by Times Offset, Malaysia

Disclaimer

The author and publishers have made every effort to ensure that all instructions given in
this book are safe and accurate, but they cannot accept liability for any resulting injury or
loss or damage to either property or person, whether direct or consequential or however
arising.

CONTENTS

Introduction 6

BAKING BASICS 8
  Equipment 10
  Types of Tins (Pans) 14
  Lining Tins (Pans) 15
  Lining Frames 16
  Lining Novelty Tins (Pans) 16
  Before Baking the Cake 17
  Special Dietary Needs 18

THE CAKE ITSELF 20
  Fruit Cake 22
  Sponge Cake 23

PERFECT CAKE COVERINGS 28
  Working with Marzipan 30
  Working with Sugarpaste
    (Rolled Fondant or Ready
    to Roll Icing) 32

SIMPLE DECORATING
TECHNIQUES 46
  Ribbons 48
  Sausage Edges 51
  Texture 52
  Twisted Edges 52
  Stippling 55
  Embossing 56
  Crimping 57
  Cut-Outs 58
  Inserts 59
  Quilling 60
  Painting 61

ADVANCED DECORATING
TECHNIQUES 62
  Frills 64
  Piping 66
  Special Effects 78
  Modelling 84

EASY TIERED WEDDING
CAKES 100
  Tiered Wedding Cakes 102
  Using a Cake Stand 102
  Using Pillars 103
  Using a Separator 105
  Making Stacked
    Cakes 106

THE ESSENTIALS 107
  Storage and
    Transportation 108
  Cutting Cakes 108
  Portion Guide 109
  Recipes 111

Index 126

INTRODUCTION

Decorating a cake – whether it is a child's party cake or a sugarcraft masterpiece – is a skill anyone can master with a little practice. It really is fun, and all you need to do is learn a few of the basics.

Throughout my many years in the cake-decorating business, I have often been asked to write down my experiences. That is exactly what I have done here – and believe me; I have included all of my secrets! This book takes you back to the beginning. It covers essential equipment, methods for lining tins (pans), delicious cake recipes (including several that are suitable for people with food allergies and intolerances) and step-by-step instructions for decorating your cakes in dozens of different ways.

Each chapter includes invaluable hints, plus all of the information you need to successfully make and decorate a cake for a special occasion. Enjoy the book and happy cake decorating.

CHAPTER ONE

BAKING BASICS

This section gives you all of the

information you need to know before you

start making a cake. There is useful

advice on choosing and lining various tins

(pans), plus tips on making suitable cakes

for allergy sufferers and diabetics.

Equipment

There is no need to rush out and buy everything on this list before you decorate your first cake. Generally, tins (pans), a rolling pin, sharp knives, a palette knife (metal spatula), a smoother and, if you plan to work with sugarpaste (also known as rolled fondant or ready-to-roll icing), a paintbrush will suffice. Over time, you will work out which pieces of equipment you need most, and your collection will gradually build.

Airtight bottles (4) Useful for storing the alcoholic mixture used to 'feed' fruit cakes.

Airtight containers (16) A selection of large and small containers stores ingredients between use and protects fruit cakes while they mature.

Baking trays Use with frames to prevent cake mixture from spilling out during baking.

Balling mat (13) Use with a balling tool to frill or give 'movement' to sugarpaste and Mexican paste.

Balling tool (14) Use to model shapes and figures, and to frill or give 'movement' to sugarpaste and Mexican paste.

Boards (6) Place under cakes as a finishing touch; boards should always be 7.5cm (3in) larger than cakes.

Cake wire (2) Use to slice sponge cakes in half for filling.

Cel stick (11) A slender stick with a pointed end used to model shapes and figures; usually made of durable, non-stick plastic.

Cling film (plastic wrap) (8) Use to line novelty tins and to prevent sugarpaste and marzipan from drying out.

Cocktail sticks (toothpicks) (10) Ideal for adding colour to sugarpaste and royal icing.

Cooling racks (20) Use to cool cakes.

Crimpers (1) Tweezer-like tools used to create patterns on sugarpaste.

Cutters (17) Available in a variety of shapes and sizes.

Dowels (19) Run through pillars, separators and stacked cakes to support the tiers; available in plastic and can be cut to size.

Drums (7) Thick boards that lift up cakes for decorating.

Embossers (15) Leave imprints of pictures or words when pressed into sugarpaste.

Food colouring (18) Adds colour to sugarpaste, marzipan, royal icing and buttercream; available in paste, powder and liquid forms.

Food dust Apply with a paintbrush to add colour to sugarpaste and marzipan.

Garrett frill cutter (12) Scalloped cutter that gives sugarpaste and Mexican paste frilled or scalloped edges; ones with interchangeable centres are the most versatile.

Glue stick (3) Essential for attaching decorations to boards and drums.

Greaseproof (waxed) paper (21) Use to line tins (pans) and to make piping tubes (nozzles) and templates; comes in pre-cut rolls and sheets.

Icing ruler (5) Smoothes buttercream and royal icing; usually made of metal or plastic.

Kitchen (aluminum or tin) foil (9) Adds an extra layer of protection to fruit cakes while they mature.

Kitchen paper (paper towels) Use with embossers and food dust, and to tidy up imperfections on cake coverings.

Measuring spoons (12) Ensure you use the right quantities of ingredients every time you make recipes.

Mixing bowls (7) Essential for making cake mixtures, buttercream, marzipan, sugarpaste and royal icing.

Paintbrushes (20) Use to paint and to add delicate details and food dust to marzipan, sugarpaste and Mexican paste. Also useful for dampening modelled figures before assembling them.

Palette knife (metal spatula) (19) Useful for spreading jam (jelly) and buttercream on sponge cakes, and for lifting small pieces of sugarpaste and dried royal icing.

Pillars (5) Use to separate tiers of a cake; often made of plastic and can be round, square and octagonal.

Piping (decorating) bags (3) Use with piping tubes (nozzles) to pipe royal icing; usually made of greaseproof (waxed) paper.

Piping tubes (nozzles) (1) Come in a range of sizes and shapes, including plain writing tubes and star and shell tubes (see page 66 for the most useful sizes); the metal ones last the longest.

Pizza wheel (18) Use to cut marzipan, sugarpaste and Mexican paste when crisp, clean edges are required.

Plastic bags (4) Can be wrapped round fruit cakes while they mature, and sugarpaste before use, to prevent them from drying out.

Rolling pins (14) Invaluable for rolling out marzipan, sugarpaste and Mexican paste.

Scissors (13) Use to cut linings for tins (pans) and to make piping (decorating) bags and templates.

Scriber (scalpel) (11) Essential for marking outlines on marzipan, sugarpaste and Mexican paste.

Separators (6) Use to separate tiers of a cake; available in a range of shapes and sizes.

Sharp knives (10) Use to shape and slice cakes, and to trim marzipan and sugarpaste.

Side smoother (15) Smoothes marzipan and sugarpaste round the sides of cakes.

Sieve (strainer) (9) Use to sieve (sift) flour and icing (confectioners') sugar, and to create sugarpaste special effects.

Smoother (16) Invaluable for smoothing out the lumps and bumps on marzipan and sugarpaste cake coverings.

Stands (see page 102) Useful for displaying two- to five-tier cakes; usually made of metal or Perspex.

Sugar shaker (22) Use to dust work surfaces with icing (confectioners') sugar to prevent marzipan, sugarpaste and Mexican paste from sticking and tearing.

Tape measure Measures the height and circumference of cakes; a washable variety is the best.

Tins (pans) (see page 14) An assortment of shapes and sizes comes in handy.

Turntable (2) Lifts, turns and in some cases tilts cakes, enabling you to decorate the sides with ease.

Veiner (17) Creates realistic vein effects on sugarpaste and marzipan flowers and foliage.

Wooden spoons (8) Use to stir cake mixtures.

Types of Tins (Pans)

Tins (pans) can be broken down into three categories: tins (1), frames (see page 16) and novelty tins (2). The cake you are making will determine the kind of tin you need – but don't forget that you can always hire them, thereby reducing your outlay costs.

Tins

There are all sorts of tins available for making cakes, ranging from round and square ones to petal- and oval-shaped varieties. Always go for a good, sturdy make. You will not only get a better-quality cake from it but, if you look after it, it will last for a lifetime.

If possible, avoid square tins with rounded corners. Cakes made in these tins never look good when they are covered and decorated, because their edges are not crisp enough. Tins with loose bottoms are also a poor investment as their bases warp with time, resulting in leaks. Finally, non-stick tins may seem like time savers, but their non-stick surfaces gradually wear off – requiring you to line them anyway.

Staff at most sugarcraft and cook shops will be able to help you find a suitable tin. If you make a lot of cakes, it is a good idea to buy a selection. That way, you will always have the right one to hand regardless of the

occasion. Sizes range from 10cm (4in) up to 40.5cm (16 in).

Frames

Frames, also known as number tins, have sides just like tins but no bases. This makes it easier for you to push out cakes once they have been baked. Frames often have strengthening bars if they have cut-out middle sections (e.g. zero and nine). Make sure these bars run across the tops of frames when you are lining them; otherwise you will make your job unnecessarily difficult.

Since frames are mainly used to make children's cakes – and most children dislike fruit cake – you will rarely make number fruit cakes. If you do find yourself in this position, however, use the ingredient amounts for a 20-cm (8-in) square fruit cake (see page 111) for all frames.

Novelty Tins

There is a huge selection of novelty tins, which increases yearly with each new hobby and children's television programme. Most novelty tins are American and come with instructions for decorating cakes with buttercream. Do not be put off by this.

Tools of the Trade

If you make a lot of cakes, you can buy reusable cake liners at any sugarcraft or cook shop. They come in all sizes and last for years. Large sheets, which can be cut into the shapes you require, are particularly useful. Just wash them after use, and they will be as good as new.

baking basics

Chapter Four, Simple Decorating Techniques (see page 46) explains how to decorate novelty cakes without resorting to piping tubes (nozzles) – though if you would like to give piping a try, it is explained in detail starting on page 66.

Like frames, most novelty tins are used to make children's cakes – and since most children dislike fruit cake, you will probably not make many novelty fruit cakes. This is a good thing, because most novelty tins are too weak to hold a fruit-cake mixture. But should you receive a special request for a novelty fruit cake, use the ingredient amounts for a 23-cm (9-in) square fruit cake (see page 111) for all novelty tins.

Lining Tins (Pans)

Lining tins (pans) may seem boring, but it keeps the cake mixture from sticking to the bottoms and sides of tins, and ensures your cakes turn out perfectly. When lining tins and frames, you will need plenty of good-quality greaseproof (waxed) paper, plus butter or margarine. Novelty tins, however, will require you to use cling film (plastic wrap) or flour with the butter or margarine.

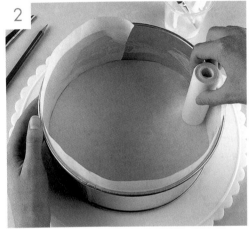

1. Place the tin on a piece of greaseproof paper of approximately the same size and draw round its base. Cut out the shape and slip it into the bottom of the tin (Fig. 1). There is no need to grease the bottom of the tin first.

Troubleshooting

Never leave tins to dry naturally. Wash them in warm, soapy water and dry them in a warm oven. This prevents them from rusting and prolongs their lives.

2. Lightly grease the sides of the tin with butter or margarine, then use a tape measure to measure the tin's height. Either use greaseproof paper on a roll that is 2.5cm (1in) wider than the height of the tin (Fig. 2) or cut a strip or greaseproof paper to this measurement to line the sides. Roll it round the inside of the tin, allowing the ends to overlap slightly.

With square tins, make sure you push the greaseproof paper right into the corners. This will make it impossible for the cake mixture to leak out and stick to the tin during baking.

15

baking basics

Lining Frames

Because of their strengthening bars and irregular shapes, frames are the trickiest kinds of tins (pans) to line. Take it slowly at first to make sure you get it right.

1. Since frames do not have bases, you will need to create them. First, set a sheet of greaseproof (waxed) paper that is at least 15cm (6in) bigger than the frame all the way round on top of a baking tray. Then position the frame upside-down – so the strengthening bar (or bars) runs across the top – on this.

2. Take the four corners of the greaseproof paper and twist them. This brings the paper up round the outside of the frame and ensures the mixture will not spill out (Fig. 1).

3. Line the sides of the frame as described in Lining Tins (Pans), step 2 (see page 15) (Fig. 2). Do not add the extra 2.5cm (1in) to the greaseproof paper's width, though, or it will be difficult to work round the supporting bar. If the frame has a cut-out section in the middle, line this in the same way as the sides.

Lining Novelty Tins (Pans)

The whole point of using novelty tins (pans) is to create cakes embossed with their detailing, so you cannot line them with greaseproof (waxed) paper or the details will be obscured. Instead, line them with cling film (plastic wrap) or a light dusting of flour, depending on your oven (see below).

Electric Ovens

First, grease the tin with butter or margarine, then line it with a generous amount of cling

Tools of the Trade

When you are lining novelty tins (pans), use a good-quality cling film (plastic wrap) that is suitable for use in the microwave to achieve the best results.

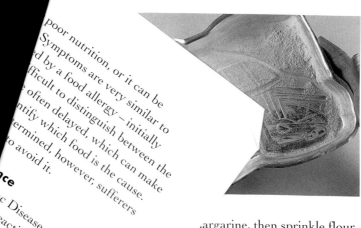

poor nutrition, or it can be
Symptoms are very similar to
...d by a food allergy – initially
...fficult to distinguish between the
... often delayed, which can make
...ntify which food is the cause.
...ermined, however, sufferers
...o avoid it.

...nce

...liac Disease (CD), gluten
... a reaction to the glutens
...ome cereals, including
...ng a cake for someone
... use only gluten-free
... You will find
...it and sponge cakes
...ch begins on page
...oth cakes with
...paste (rolled
... a recipe for
... 30, and the

... or
...kes. If
...u should
...the bottom of
...moisture in the
..., soft. Top up the
...ghout baking.

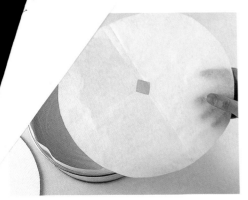

...argarine, then sprinkle flour
... the sides of the tin with your
... the entire tin an even coating of
... 2), then turn it upside down to get
...ne excess.
...f you prefer, you could use 'cake spray'
...stead of butter or margarine. It works well
and does not require you to flour the tin.

Before Baking the Cake

There are several questions you should ask
yourself and the recipient of your cake before
you start baking. Establishing the answers
well in advance will ensure that your cakes
are well received, each and every time.

▼ How many people will the cake need to
   serve?
   Once you know this, consult the Portion
   Guide on page 109. This will tell you how
   many portions of sponge cake or fruit cake
   you can expect to get from different sizes
   and types of tins (pans).

▼ What sort of cake does the recipient like?

▼ Are there any special dietary needs to
   consider?

It could be a disaster if you make a fruit cake covered in marzipan – which is packed with almonds – for someone with a nut allergy. Consult Special Dietary Needs below to find out which recipes are suitable for people suffering from food allergies, food intolerances and diabetes.

▼ Does the cake need to travel far?
Storage and Transportation on page 108 tells you everything you need to know to get your cake safely to its final destination.

▼ Is there anything you can do in advance?
Home-made marzipan should be used as soon as possible (though it is worth noting that ready-made versions keep well), but royal icing will keep for one week in an airtight container, and sugarpaste (rolled fondant or ready-to-roll icing) will keep for two. (There is no need to refrigerate royal icing or sugarpaste; just give the royal icing a good stir, and the sugarpaste a good knead, before use.) Buttercream freezes well, as do freshly baked and cooled sponge cakes, which can be frozen plain or buttercreamed for up to a month. Fruit cakes can – and really should – be baked three months before they are needed to allow the flavours to develop. Store them during this time in plastic bags or airtight containers in a cool, dark place.

You will find classic fruit and sponge cake recipes in Chapter 2, The Cake Itself (see pages 22 and 23) and variations in Recipes, which starts on page 111.

Special Dietary Needs

Food intolerances

A food intolerance is a condition in which a person has an adverse reaction to a particular food. It can be caused by the lack of an enzyme needed to digest the food, stress,

illness o
inherited.
those caus
making it d
two – and ar
it tricky to ide
Once this is de
are encouraged

Gluten Intolerd

Also known as Coe
intolerance involves
or proteins found in
wheat. If you are mak
with gluten intolerance
baking powder and flou
recipes for gluten-free fr
in the Recipes section, wh
111. Feel free to decorate b
ordinary marzipan and suga
fondant or ready-to-roll icing
marzipan can be found on pag
sugarpaste recipe is on page 32

Food Allergies

Unlike a food intolerance, a food a
involves the immune system. Durin
allergic reaction, the immune system
mistakes a harmless food as a threat.
creates chemicals and histamines in an
attempt to protect the body, which trigg
symptoms that affect the skin, respiratory
system, gastrointestinal tract and
cardiovascular system. Symptoms arise
within minutes of eating or touching a
particular food, so allergy sufferers must
avoid it at all times.

Egg Allergy

Generally, it is the proteins found in egg
whites (albumen) that cause a reaction in
someone with an egg allergy, but proteins in
the yolks can also cause problems.

baking basics

It is essential that you eliminate all eggs and egg products from any cake you make for an egg-allergy sufferer. You will find recipes for egg-free fruit and sponge cakes and marzipan, and albumen-free royal icing, in the Recipes section, which starts on page 111. If you plan to use ready-made sugarpaste (rolled fondant or ready-to-roll icing), be sure to check the ingredients list beforehand, as some brands contain egg whites. (The recipe in this book, which can be found on page 32, does not.)

Nut Allergy

Ordinary marzipan, which contains almonds, is off limits for those with a nut allergy. If you must cover a fruit cake that you have made for a nut-allergy sufferer, either replace the marzipan with nut-free marzipan (see page 123) or apply a thin layer of sugarpaste (rolled fondant or ready-to-roll icing) and proceed as normal. You will find the recipe for ordinary sugarpaste on page 32.

Dairy Allergy

This is the most common type of food allergy and requires sufferers to give up all foods containing cow's milk, such as cheese and butter. The Recipes section, which starts on page 111, includes recipes for a dairy-free fruit cake, sponge cake and chocolate topping.

E-Number Allergy

E numbers represent colours, preservatives, additives and other agents that are included in packaged goods. They have been tested for safety and passed in the European Community but still cause allergic reactions in some people. If you are making a cake for someone who is allergic to a particular E number, check the ingredients lists on all of the products you are using to make sure they are safe.

Thinking Ahead

Whenever you are making a cake for someone with a food intolerance or allergy, make sure you thoroughly wash all surfaces and equipment before you begin. Never just carry on and ice a cake for a nut-allergy sufferer with the same rolling pin that you have been using to apply marzipan to another cake, for example.

Diabetes

Diabetes arises when the body either cannot produce insulin (a hormone that regulates the amount of glucose, or sugar, in the blood) or cannot use the insulin it produces. There are no foods that diabetics should avoid, and there is no need to cut out all sugar if you are making a cake for someone who has the disease. Like everyone, however, people with diabetes should try to eat only small amounts of foods that are high in sugar or fat. You will find low-sugar and low-fat fruit and sponge cake recipes in the Recipes section, which starts on page 111. If you are making a sponge cake for a diabetic, be sure to use only diabetic jam (jelly) and cream filling (see recipe, page 120; the sugar content in ordinary buttercream recipes is far too high for someone with the disease). If you are intent on covering the cake, give it a very thin layer of sugarpaste (rolled fondant or ready-to-roll icing) and suggest the recipient removes it before eating the cake. You will find the recipe for ordinary sugarpaste on page 32.

CHAPTER TWO

THE CAKE ITSELF

In the excitement to get to the most glamorous part of making a cake – decorating it – it is tempting to rush through the preceding steps. But if your cake is to look and taste as good as you want it to, you must master the recipes for classic fruit and sponge cakes, and the all-essential techniques of levelling, cutting and filling cakes.

Fruit Cake

Nothing beats the rich aroma of fruits and spices that wafts through the house when a fruit cake is baking. It is the ideal winter warmer.

The only drawback to making a fruit cake is that it should ideally be baked three months before it is needed to give the flavours plenty of time to develop. (The Timesaving Tip below offers a shortcut, however.) Fruit cake is also rather high maintenance after baking, requiring a big 'drink' of alcoholic mixture – drizzle 60 ml (4 tbsp) over a 20-cm (8-in) cake – immediately after it comes out of the oven, followed by a series of smaller 'drinks' – drizzle over roughly 15ml (3 tbsp) – every one to two weeks thereafter.

After you have given your fruit cake its first big 'drink', wrap the cake in two layers of greaseproof (waxed) paper, then wrap it loosely in a plastic bag or put it into an airtight container. Never wrap a fruit cake straight into kitchen (aluminium or tin) foil; the fruit reacts with the foil, and the cake eventually takes on a metallic taste. Store it in a cool, dark place, only removing it to give the cake its small 'drinks' every week or so.

Feeding Fruit Cakes

A mixture of alcohol, glycerine and hot water makes for a lovely, moist cake. Each time you make a fruit cake, blend a fresh batch made up of two parts alcohol, one part glycerine and one part hot water, and store it in an airtight bottle until you need it. Substitute this mixture with pineapple juice if you are making a fruit cake for someone who does not like the flavour of alcohol.

Timesaving Tip

If you are short of time and need a fruit cake quickly, wrap it in greaseproof (waxed) paper after you have fed it and it has cooled down, and put it in the freezer. Freeze the cake for a minimum of 24 hours, then defrost it at room temperature for another 24 hours at least. This helps with the maturing process and draws out the flavours. Once the cake has defrosted, you can continue with the marzipan stage (see Working with Marzipan, page 30).

Making a Fruit Cake

INGREDIENTS

(See Fruit Cake, page 111, for specific amounts and recommended baking temperature and times)

> Glacé (candied) cherries, chopped
> Currants
> Sultanas (golden raisins)
> Raisins
> Mixed fruit peel
> Lemon rind, grated
> Plain (all-purpose) flour
> Almonds, chopped
> Ground cinnamon
> Nutmeg
> Mixed (pumpkin pie) spice
> Butter or margarine
> Brown sugar
> Eggs
> Black treacle (molasses)

METHOD

1. Put the cherries in a mixing bowl with the currants, sultanas (golden raisins), raisins, mixed fruit peel and lemon rind.

2. In a separate bowl, blend the plain (all-purpose) flour, almonds, ground cinnamon, nutmeg and mixed (pumpkin pie) spice.

3. Cream the butter/margarine until it is light, fluffy and white in colour. Add the brown sugar and mix a little further.

4. Add the eggs, one at a time, to the butter, with a little of the flour mixture.

5. Stir in the remaining flour mixture and the dried fruit.

6. Add the black treacle (molasses) and blend.

7. Spoon the mixture into a lined tin (pan) and make a slight depression in the centre of the mixture. This helps to keep the cake level as it bakes.

8. After baking, feed the cake and either freeze it for 24 hours (see Timesaving Tip, opposite) for immediate use, or wrap it in two layers of greaseproof (waxed) paper and store it in a plastic bag or airtight container for three months (see Fruit Cake, left).

Sponge cake

Quick to make, sponge cake is the ideal option if you need to make a cake with little advance notice. It has a short shelf life, so it should only be covered and decorated a few days before it is going to be eaten. (Thinking Ahead, above, offers a way around this, however.)

It is possible to extend the life of a sponge cake by adding a small amount of glycerine to the recipe. You could also substitute part of the self-raising (self-rising) flour with ground almonds. A good rule of thumb is to substitute approximately 25g (1oz) of every 225g (8oz/2 cups) of flour with ground almonds. Whichever method you use, bear in mind that the

Thinking Ahead

Though a sponge cake must be covered and decorated just before it is going to be eaten, the cake itself can be made and frozen up to a month in advance. When you are ready to use it, defrost the cake at room temperature, which should take a couple of hours, then wrap it in greaseproof (waxed) paper until you are able to begin decorating.

cake's life will be extended by only a few days, depending on the season (its shelf life is much shorter in the summer) and where it is stored. Cakes always last longer if they are kept in a cool, dark place.

Making a Sponge Cake

INGREDIENTS

(see Sponge Cake, page 115, for specific amounts and recommended baking temperature and times)

Butter or margarine
Caster (superfine) sugar
Eggs
Self-raising (self-rising) flour
Milk or water

METHOD

1. In a mixing bowl, blend together the butter/margarine and the caster (superfine) sugar until the mixture is light and fluffy.

2. Break the eggs into a separate mixing bowl and whisk them with a fork.

3. Alternately pour the eggs and the self-raising (self-rising) flour into the butter mixture, then fold it together with a spoon.

23

4. Gradually add the milk/water to the mixture to soften its consistency.

5. Spoon the mixture into a lined tin (pan) and make a slight depression in the centre of the mixture. This helps to keep the cake level as it bakes.

6. After baking, use the cake immediately or freeze it either plain or buttercreamed for up to one month (see Thinking Ahead, page 23).

Levelling Sponge Cakes

Cakes are always covered with a sheet of sugarpaste (rolled fondant or ready-to-roll icing) before they are decorated. Unfortunately, any bumps or gaps in the cake will be highlighted by the covering, so it is essential that the top of the cake is perfectly smooth.

The easiest way to achieve this is to turn the tin (pan) upside down onto a clean board (see Cutting Sponge Cakes in Half, opposite) to release the cake. This prevents you from having to 'lever' the cake out of the tin, potentially damaging it, and gives you a nice, smooth top to decorate later. But what do you do if the top of the cake (now the bottom) is uneven and the cake will not sit flat on the board?

1. Place the cake back in the tin, with the uneven surface facing upwards.

2. Slide a sharp knife across the top of the tin, frame or novelty tin (Figs 1, 2 and 3). When you turn out the cake, it will be level on both the top and the bottom.

If the cake does not rise to the top of the tin, put a small drum inside the tin and set the cake on top of this. The cake should now sit high enough for you to level it.

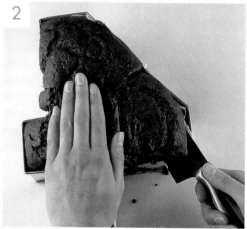

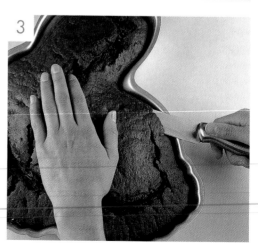

24

Cutting Sponge Cakes in Half

Classic sponge cakes are sliced in half, then filled with buttercream and a jam (jelly) glaze, which is essentially watered-down jam that is then reduced to a glaze (see recipe, page 30). Many novices saw through the cake with a knife, more often than not ending up with two halves that resemble steeply angled ski slopes.

You can avoid this by following either of the two methods outlined below. Before you get started, place the cake on a board that has been thoroughly cleaned with kitchen paper (paper towels) and Isopropyl Alcohol (IPA) (Fig. 1), which you can find at any sugarcraft or cook shop. This cleans away dirt particles or bacteria that may have gathered on the board and prevents the growth of mould between the cake and the board. If you cannot find IPA, use any white alcohol, gin or vodka. Warm, previously boiled water will also do.

Method One

Position the cake and board on a turntable. Horizontally embed the knife midway up the cake with one hand and place your other hand on top of the cake to hold it in position. Keeping the point of the knife in the same position all the time, use the hand that is holding the top of the cake to gently rotate the turntable. You will be able to see what you are doing and will know where the point of the knife is at all times (Fig. 2). Slip a thin, 4-mm (¼-in) board beneath the top half of the cake, ease the cake onto it (Fig. 3), then set it aside.

Method Two

Again, position the cake and board on a turntable, though this is not essential. Wrap a cake wire round the cake halfway down the sides. Hold the ends of the wire in one hand

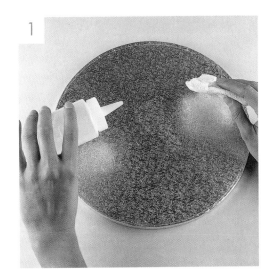

25

4

Filling Sponge Cakes

Fillings are a matter of personal choice, but many people opt to use classic buttercream, which keeps well in the refrigerator for up to one month.

Making Buttercream

INGREDIENTS

(see page 121 for specific amounts)

Butter or margarine
Icing (confectioners') sugar
Hot water

METHOD

1. Cream the butter/margarine in a mixing bowl until it is almost white in colour.

2. Stir in the icing (confectioners') sugar a little at a time.

3. Continue stirring in the icing sugar and gradually add the water. (The main purpose of the water in this recipe is to soften the consistency of the buttercream if necessary.)

4. Blend until the buttercream has a smooth, spreading consistency.

5. Use the buttercream immediately or freeze it in a plastic bag or airtight container for up to a month. Give it a thorough stir just before use.

and place your other hand on top of the cake to hold it in position. Pull the wire through the cake, keeping your hand at the same level all the time (Fig. 4). If you do not have a cake wire, take a length of fine food grade wire, wrap each end round a dowel, then tape over it. This will prevent the wire from moving. Lift the top half of the cake with a thin, 4-mm (¼-in) board, as in Method One.

Tools of the Trade

If you cannot find cake wire, use a length of plain dental floss. Wrap it round your fingers or tie it round two dowels, then proceed as for the cake wire (see above). This is a very hygienic way of cutting a cake, because the dental floss is disposable.

If you are filling a cake with both jam (jelly) and buttercream, remove the top half of the cake, leaving the bottom half and board on a turntable, as described in Cutting Sponge Cakes in Half, page 25. Use a palette knife (metal spatula) to spread the buttercream on the bottom half of the cake, then top this with the jam (Fig. 1).

26

the cake itself

Avoid putting on too much of any filling, because it will ooze out when the top of the cake is set in place. Do not worry if the filling does not initially go right up to the edges of the cake. You will find that the weight of the cake's top half will spread it out, and the whole cake will have plenty of filling when it is cut.

To put the top half of the cake back in position, pick up the board and tilt it until the cake is perfectly centred on the bottom half (Fig. 2). Press the top half down gently with your hand. Spread a thin layer of buttercream on the top and sides of the cake with one hand, using your other hand to gently rotate the turntable (Fig. 3). The buttercream coating will act as a masking to which the sugarpaste (rolled fondant or ready-to-roll icing) covering, which you will add later, will stick.

27

the cake itself

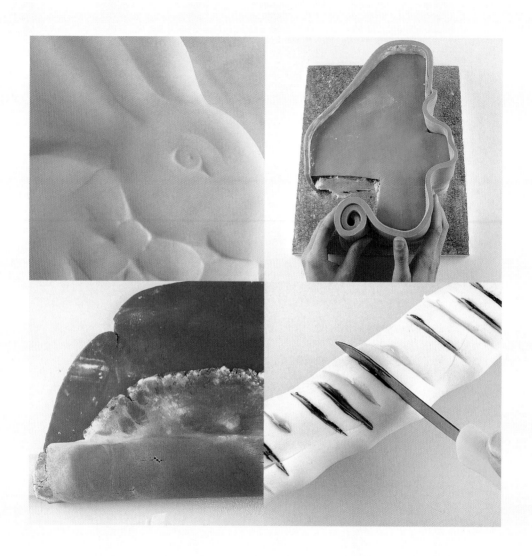

CHAPTER THREE

PERFECT CAKE COVERINGS

Your cake has now been baked, levelled, cut and filled to perfection. It is time to think about the covering, which will seal the cake and create a smooth surface for any decorations you may choose to add. This chapter takes you through the two different types of coverings – marzipan and sugarpaste (rolled fondant or ready-to-roll icing) – and explains how to cover boards and cakes.

Working with Marzipan

Both sponge and fruit cakes are covered with sugarpaste (rolled fondant or ready-to-roll icing), but fruit cakes are first given a coating of jam (jelly) glaze (see recipe, right) and marzipan to lock in moisture. Marzipan is made primarily of ground almonds and two types of sugar.

Making Marzipan

INGREDIENTS

(see page 121 for specific amounts)
    Ground almonds
    Icing (confectioners') sugar
    Caster (superfine) sugar
    Egg yolks
    Rum or brandy (optional)

METHOD

1. In a mixing bowl, blend together the ground almonds, icing (confectioners') sugar and caster (superfine) sugar.

2. Add the egg yolks and the rum or brandy, if used.

3. Knead the mixture – but do not over-knead or it will become oily – and use immediately.

Tools of the Trade

Many people assume they must use apricot jam (jelly) for the jam glaze. This was certainly the case in the early days of cake decorating, when other jams contained vast amounts of food colouring – but now you can use any flavour of jam you like.

Making a Jam (Jelly) Glaze

INGREDIENTS
    Boiling water
    Jam (jelly)

METHOD

1. Add 30ml (2 tbsp) of boiling water to approximately 60ml (4 tbsp) of jam (jelly) and blend.

2. Put the mixture in the microwave or heat it in a bowl set over a saucepan of boiling water.

3. Bring the mixture to boiling point, then remove it from the heat and use immediately.

Covering Sponge Cakes with Marzipan

Cake decorators sometimes apply an initial layer of marzipan to sponge cakes because they feel it gives them a smoother base for the sugarpaste covering. This should not be necessary if you have levelled the cake correctly (see page 24). If you feel you need an extra coating of some sort, however – and know that marzipan is not suitable for the recipient of the cake – replace the marzipan with a thin layer of sugarpaste, let it crust, then add the sugarpaste covering as normal.

Covering Fruit Cakes with Marzipan

Before you get started, make sure you have the correct quantity of marzipan (see Marzipan Guide, page 110). If you only have enough to apply a thin layer to the cake, the subsequent sugarpaste covering will have a poor finish.

If you decide to buy ready-made marzipan, buy the best-quality brand you can find. Cheaper versions are difficult to knead and often end up cracking on the corners of the cake. Always use white marzipan which, unlike the yellow version, does not contain any added colouring.

1. Position the fruit cake in the centre of a cleaned board (see Cutting Sponge Cakes in Half, page 25). If there is a gap between the cake and the board, fill it with marzipan pieces. Do not worry too much about air holes or small spaces where pieces of fruit have dropped out.

2. Knead the marzipan on a clean work surface until you have achieved a smooth, crack-free paste. This may take a little while (Fig. 1).

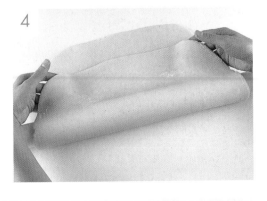

3. Using a palette knife (metal spatula), spread the jam glaze all over the top and sides of the cake (Fig. 2).

4. Place the marzipan on a work surface lightly dusted with icing (confectioners') sugar and roll it out to a thin layer – though no thinner than 8mm (⅜in). Try to keep the marzipan roughly the same shape as the cake, allowing enough to cover its top and sides. If the marzipan has rolled out into an awkward shape, do not be afraid to knock it back into shape with the side of the rolling pin.

5. Go over the marzipan with a smoother (Fig. 3) so that when you run your hand over it, you cannot feel any ridges.

6. Place the rolling pin in the middle of the marzipan. Pick up two 'corners' and quickly flip this half of the marzipan over the rolling pin (Fig. 4).

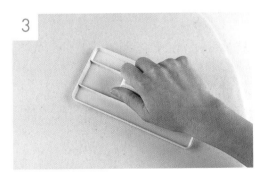

7. Lift up the rolling pin and position the marzipan against one side of the cake. Rotate the rolling pin to flip the marzipan over the cake (Fig. 5). Touching it with your fingers

31

at this stage will leave marks and indentations – a shame after all the effort you have just put into smoothing it.

8. Using the palms of your hands, smooth the marzipan from the centre of the cake outwards to expel any trapped air. Gently ease the marzipan in round the sides of the cake, again using the palms of your hands. Go over the sides of the cake with a side smoother.

9. Trim away any excess marzipan from the base of the cake with a sharp knife held completely straight. Glide it through the marzipan; a sawing motion would leave jagged edges. Using the palms of your hands, smooth the marzipan round the base of the cake to create a seal between the cake and the board (Fig. 6).

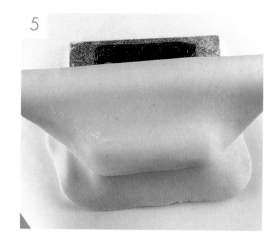

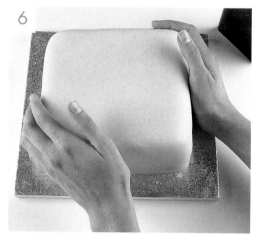

Working With Sugarpaste (Rolled Fondant or Ready-to-Roll Icing)

Sugarpaste, also known as rolled fondant or ready-to-roll icing, contains icing (confectioners') sugar, gelatine and glucose, and is used to cover boards, sponge cakes and marzipanned fruit cakes to give them a smooth finish for further decorating.

Making your own sugarpaste is not difficult, but it is perfectly acceptable to use ready-made versions. Most are suitable for vegetarians and vegans, though you may need to check their ingredients lists if you are making a cake for someone who is allergic to E numbers. Always buy ready-made sugarpaste from sugarcraft or cook shops, because the quality of those sold at supermarkets varies widely.

Making Sugarpaste

INGREDIENTS
(see page 124 for specific amounts)

Icing (confectioners') sugar
Rose water, lemon juice or kirsch (optional)
Water
Powdered gelatine
Liquid glucose

METHOD
1. Sieve (sift) the icing (confectioners') sugar into a large mixing bowl. Stir in the rose water, lemon juice or kirsch, if used.

2. Spoon the water into a separate bowl or saucepan. Sprinkle over the powdered gelatine and leave it to 'sponge' in the water.

3. Gently heat the gelatine mixture in the microwave or over the hob (stove), but do not allow it to boil.

4. Stir most of the icing sugar into the gelatine mixture one spoonful at a time. When it begins to stiffen, knead in the remaining icing sugar. You may find it is easier to turn out the mixture onto a work surface before you do this.

5. Put the mixture in a plastic bag and remove all of the air. Leave it for 24 hours before use, and use it within two weeks. There is no need to refrigerate sugarpaste; simply give it a good knead before use.

Kneading Sugarpaste

Kneading is the most important stage when you are working with sugarpaste and should be done on a clean work surface. If you knead on icing (confectioners') sugar, you will only end up kneading the sugar into the sugarpaste, which will make it dry out faster and later cause the edges of your cake covering to crack. Always knead sugarpaste until it has a smooth consistency. Because it hardens as it is exposed to air, wrap any sugarpaste that you will not be using immediately in cling film (plastic wrap). It does not need to be stored in the refrigerator.

Covering Cakes and Boards with Sugarpaste

(THE ALL-IN-ONE METHOD)

This is the ideal method if you want your cake and board to be covered with a single colour of sugarpaste. If you would prefer that the board is a different colour, however,

you will need to cover it 48 hours in advance (see page 40) and cover your cake separately.

Do not forget that, before you begin, sponge cakes should already be covered with buttercream (see Filling Sponge Cakes, page 26), and fruit cakes with marzipan that has been dampened with a little previously boiled water, gin or vodka. The cleaned board (see Cutting Sponge Cakes in Half, page 25) should also be dampened with a little previously boiled water, or the sugarpaste covering will not stick. Consult the Sugarpaste Guide on page 110 to make sure you have enough sugarpaste.

1. Place the kneaded sugarpaste (see left) on a surface lightly dusted with icing (confectioners') sugar and roll it out until it is approximately 1cm (½in) thick. Try to keep the sugarpaste roughly the same shape as the cake and board. If it has rolled out into an awkward shape, do not be afraid to knock it back into shape with the side of the rolling pin (Fig. 1).

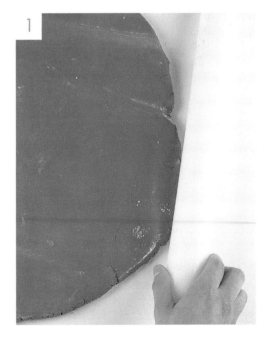

perfect cake coverings

Thinking Ahead

If you end up with excess sugarpaste (rolled fondant or ready-to-roll icing), wrap it in cling film (plastic wrap), put it in a plastic bag, then place it in the freezer. Be sure to label it with the date on which you made it. Home-made sugarpaste keeps for up to two weeks.

2. Keep turning the sugarpaste to prevent it from sticking to the work surface. If you find it is becoming more difficult to turn as it is rolled out, flip it over the rolling pin and gently lift it, sprinkling a little icing sugar on the work surface (Fig. 2). Continue rolling out the sugarpaste until it is wide enough to comfortably cover the cake and the top of the board.

3. When you have finished rolling out the sugarpaste, go over it with a smoother to remove any ridges.

4. Place the rolling pin in the middle of the sugarpaste. Pick up two 'corners' and quickly flip this half of the sugarpaste over the rolling pin.

5. Lift up the rolling pin and position the sugarpaste against one side of the board. Rotate the rolling pin to flip the sugarpaste over the cake and board, without touching it with your hands. Touching it with your fingers at this stage will leave marks and indentations – a shame after all the effort you have just put into smoothing it.

6. Using the palms of your hands, smooth the sugarpaste on the top of the cake, moving from the centre of the cake outwards to expel any trapped air. Then, go over the cake's top with the smoother. How you deal with the sides depends on the cake's shape (see pages 35 to 39).

Covering Round and Oval Cakes with Sugarpaste

The following steps describe how to cover a cake and board at the same time. If you have already covered the board (see page 40) and

Timesaving Tip

If you have bought several small packets of ready-made sugarpaste (rolled fondant or ready-to-roll icing), open as many as necessary, cut the required amount of sugarpaste onto the work surface and knead it all together.

perfect cake coverings

just want to cover the cake, roll out only enough sugarpaste for the cake and disregard any instructions for covering the board. After setting the cake in place on the board, you may need to go over its sides with a smoother once again to remove any nicks or scratches.

1. Roll out enough kneaded sugarpaste to cover the cake and the board and place it in position, as described in Covering Cakes and Boards with Sugarpaste (see page 33).

2. Once the top is completed, gently ease the sugarpaste round the sides of the cake and over the top of the board, using the palms of your hands to expel any trapped air.

3. Go over the sides with a side smoother (Fig. 1).

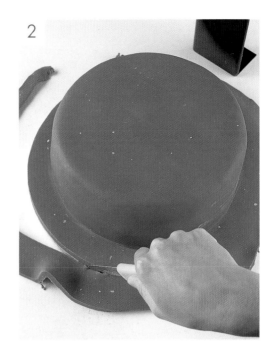

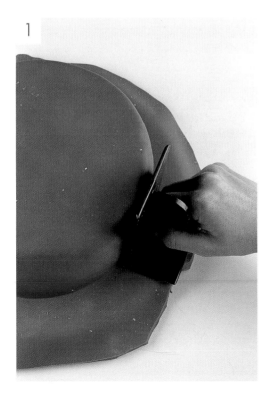

4. Trim away any excess sugarpaste by positioning a sharp knife, held completely straight, against the edge of the board. Glide it through the sugarpaste; a sawing motion would leave jagged edges (Fig. 2).

Covering Square and Hexagonal Cakes with Sugarpaste

The following steps describe how to cover a cake and board at the same time. If you have already covered the board (see page 40) and just want to cover the cake, roll out only enough sugarpaste for the cake and disregard any instructions for covering the board. After setting the cake in place on the board, you may need to go over its sides with a smoother once again to remove any nicks or scratches.

1. Roll out enough sugarpaste to cover the cake and board and place it in position, as described in Covering Cakes and Boards with Sugarpaste (see page 33).

1

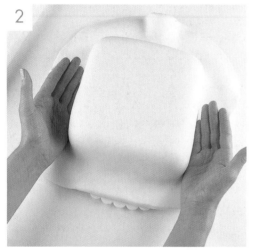

2

3

2. Once the top is completed, gently pull the sugarpaste away from the corners of the cake with your fingers and spread it out (Fig. 1).

3. Using the palms of your hands rather than your fingers, which could leave marks, start easing the sugarpaste into position on the corners of the cake. Work your way round the sides of the cake and the top of the board, expelling any trapped air. Finally, go round the base of the cake using the palms of your hands (Fig. 2). This creates a seal between the cake and the board, and prevents the cake from drying out.

4. Go over the sides of the cake with a side smoother (Fig. 3).

5. Trim away any excess sugarpaste by positioning a sharp knife, held completely straight, against the edge of the board. Glide it through the sugarpaste; a sawing motion would leave jagged edges.

Covering Number Cakes with Sugarpaste

It is not possible to cover number cakes and boards at the same time. Either leave the board as it is or cover another board 48 hours in advance in the same – or a contrasting – colour of sugarpaste (see page 40).

Tools of the Trade

Try using a till roll, which you can buy at any office-supply shop, instead of a tape measure to measure the height and circumference of a number cake. The paper can be marked up with with a pencil, then disposed of afterwards.

perfect cake coverings

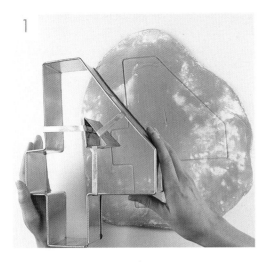

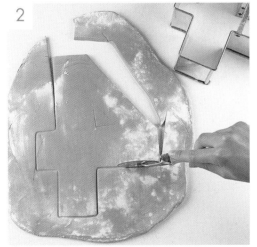

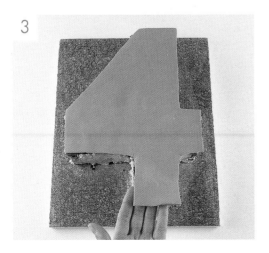

1. Roll out at least enough sugarpaste to cover the cake, as described in Covering Cakes and Boards with Sugarpaste, steps 1 to 3 (see page 33).

2. Imprint the sugarpaste with the frame in which the cake was baked, holding it upside down so the strengthening bars do not leave marks in the sugarpaste (Fig. 1).

3. Cut along the embossed outlines with a pizza wheel, which gives a nice, crisp finish (Fig. 2).

4. Place the rolling pin in the middle of the cut-out sugarpaste number. Pick up two 'corners' and quickly flip this half of the sugarpaste over the rolling pin.

5. Position the bottom of the cut-out number against the same point on the top of the cake, then rotate the rolling pin to flip the rest of the sugarpaste over the cake (Fig. 3). Go over the sugarpaste with a smoother to expel any trapped air and to give it a good finish.

6. With your hands, roll the remaining sugarpaste into a sausage shape, then go over it with the rolling pin until it has formed a long, thin strip approximately 1cm (½in) thick.

7. Using a tape measure, measure the cake's height and circumference to get a rough idea of the amount of sugarpaste you will need to

Troubleshooting

If the sugarpaste (rolled fondant or ready-to-roll icing) starts to crack on the corners of a square or hexagonal cake, rub out the cracks using the palms of your hands.

perfect cake coverings

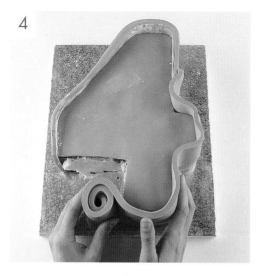

4

cover its sides. Use a pizza wheel to cut the sugarpaste to fit these measurements.

8. Loosely roll up the sugarpaste and place it at the starting point on the cake. This will either be a straight side of the cake if it has one, or a point that you have decided will be the back of the cake. Roll the sugarpaste round the cake, gently pressing it into the cake as you go so it sticks (Fig. 4), and letting the ends overlap.

9. Using a small knife, cut through the overlapping pieces. Take off the top section, then lift and remove the piece underneath it. You should find that you can butt the two ends together for a perfect join (Fig 5).

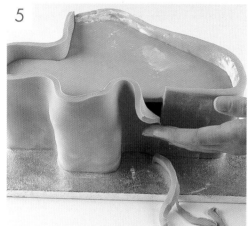

5

10. Go over the sides of the cake with a side smoother and, using the knife, trim off any excess sugarpaste from the top of the cake (Fig. 6).

11. Using two fingers, gently smooth the top edges of the sugarpaste (Fig. 7). Leave the sugarpaste to dry for 24 hours, then finish it with some piped royal icing or a sausage edge applied round the base of the cake (see Piping, page 66, and Sausage

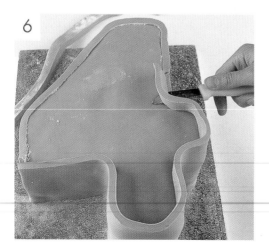

6

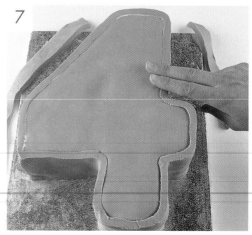

7

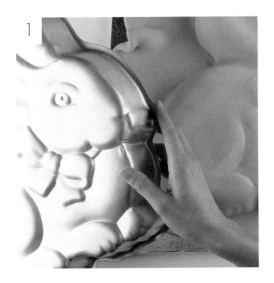

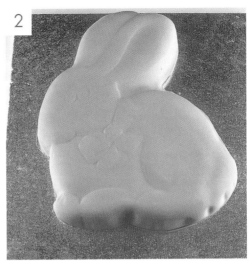

Edges, page 51). If you choose to place the cake on a previously covered board, you may need to go over its sides with a smoother once again to remove any nicks or scratches.

Covering Novelty Cakes with Sugarpaste

Novelty cakes are the easist types of cakes to cover and introduce you to basic embossing (see page 56). You can cover the cake and board at the same time, cover the board 48 hours in advance in the same – or a contrasting – colour (see page 40) or simply leave the board as it is.

1. Roll out at least enough sugarpaste to cover the cake and the board and set it in position, as described in Covering Cakes and Boards with Sugarpaste, steps 1 to 5 (see page 33).

2. Take the clean novelty tin (pan) and press it down on top of the sugarpaste to emboss the detailing. Gently lift off the tin (Fig. 1).

3. Using a sharp knife held completely straight, trim off any excess sugarpaste

approximately 1.5cm (⅝in) from the base of the cake. (Glide the knife through the sugarpaste; a sawing motion would produce a jagged edge.) This will leave you with a 0.5-cm (¼-in) ridge (Fig. 2) that you can finish in a number of ways.

The easiest way to finish the cake is to roll the remaining sugarpaste into a long, thin sausage with your hands. Moisten the ridge with a little previously boiled water and press the sausage on top of it and run it all the way round the cake. Alternatively, you could crimp the ridge or add some texture (see Crimping, page 57, and Texture, page 52).

Troubleshooting

You may find that it is easier to cover the sides of a number cake using two strips of sugarpaste (rolled fondant or ready-to-roll icing), as shown in Fig. 4, opposite. If you prefer this method, make sure the two strips overlap at the back of the cake – or at a point that will not be too visible.

perfect cake coverings

Covering Boards with Sugarpaste

Most people cover their cakes and boards at the same time (see page 33). However, sometimes covering the board with a different colour of sugarpaste gives your cake that extra 'oomph'. Just remember to give yourself plenty of time; boards must be covered at least 48 hours before cakes are set in place, or they may be marked with fingerprints, scratches or indentations.

Before you get started, make sure you have a clean board and the correct amount of sugarpaste (see Cutting Sponge Cakes in Half, page 25, and the Sugarpaste Guide, page 110). Gather together your materials and equipment, which should include a cup of previously boiled water and a paintbrush. You will need these to dampen the board before you cover it with sugarpaste, or the sugarpaste will not stick.

1. Place the kneaded sugarpaste (see page 33) on a work surface lightly dusted with icing (confectioners') sugar and roll it out until it is approximately 1cm (½in) thick. Try to keep the sugarpaste roughly the same shape as the top of the board. If it has rolled out into an awkward shape, do not be afraid to knock it back into shape with the side of the rolling pin.

2. Keep turning the sugarpaste to prevent it from sticking to the work surface. If you find it is becoming more difficult to turn as it is rolled out, flip it over the rolling pin and sprinkle a little icing sugar on the work surface. Continue rolling out the sugarpaste until it is wide enough to comfortably cover the board.

3. Go over the sugarpaste with a smoother so that when you run your hand over it, you cannot feel any ridges.

4. Using a paintbrush, brush some of the previously boiled water over the cake board to dampen it.

5. Place the rolling pin in the middle of the sugarpaste. Pick up two 'corners' and quickly flip this half of the sugarpaste over the rolling pin.

6. Lift up the rolling pin and position the sugarpaste against one side of the board. Rotate the rolling pin to flip the sugarpaste over the board. Touching it with your fingers at this stage will leave marks and indentations – a shame after all the effort you have just put into smoothing it.

7. Using the palms of your hands, smooth the sugarpaste from the centre of the board outwards to expel any trapped air (Fig. 1). Gently ease the sugarpaste in round the sides of the board, again using the palms of your hands.

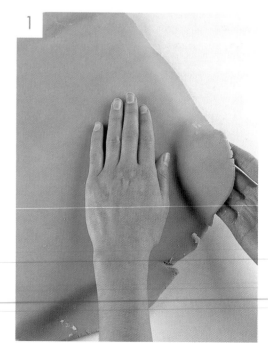

1

perfect cake coverings

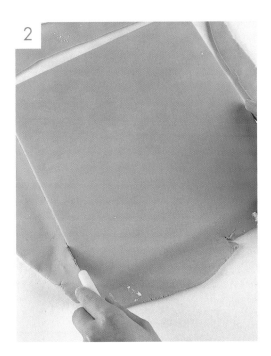

2

9. Go over the edges of the board with the smoother (Fig. 3), then set the board aside to dry for approximately 48 hours before placing the covered cake in position. If you set the cake in place any earlier than this, you risk damaging the covered board.

Colouring Sugarpaste

You can buy a vast array of coloured, ready-made sugarpaste at any sugarcraft or cook shop, but it is very easy to make your own.

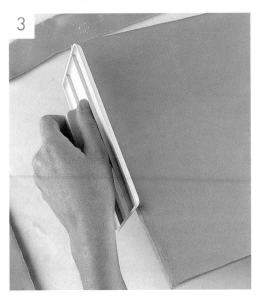

1

8. Go over the sugarpaste with the smoother, then trim away any excess sugarpaste by positioning a sharp knife, held completely straight, against the edge of the board. Glide it through the sugarpaste; a sawing motion would leave jagged edges (Fig. 2).

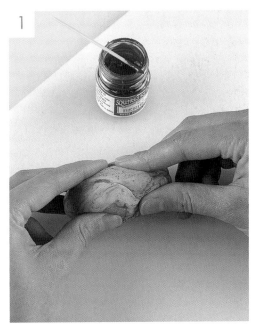

3

Before you begin, make sure you have the right quantity of white or ivory sugarpaste (see Sugarpaste Guide, page 110). Then, take the amount of sugarpaste that you wish to colour and cut off a piece the size of a table-tennis (ping-pong) ball. Apply dabs of food colouring – paste varieties are usually best – to it with a cocktail stick (toothpick) and knead the sugarpaste until it is far darker than you will ultimately require (Fig. 1).

41

2

Once the colour is evenly distributed throughout the sugarpaste, start kneading in the rest of the sugarpaste a little at a time (Fig. 2) until you have the shade you want.

Sometimes, it will not be possible to buy the exact shade of ready-made sugarpaste that you require, and you will not have the time to make your own. In these instances, you can buy existing colours of sugarpaste and combine them to create the desired shade. Before you get started, it is important to have a basic understanding of the colour wheel.

The Colour Wheel

This diagram, first designed by Sir Isaac Newton in the 1600s, is made up of primary, secondary and tertiary colours. The primary colours are red, blue and yellow (1, 5 and 9). They are the three basic colours from which all other colours are made and cannot be created by mixing any other colours together.

Tools of the Trade

Always buy concentrated food colouring at sugarcraft or cook shops. The liquid food colouring available at supermarkets is far too weak, and the liquid will change the consistency of your sugarpaste (rolled fondant or ready-to-roll icing).

The secondary colours are purple, green and orange (3, 7 and 11 on the colour wheel) and are created by mixing equal parts of two primary colours. Mixing red (1) and blue (5), for instance, makes purple (3); mixing blue (5) and yellow (9) makes green (7); and mixing yellow (9) and red (1) makes orange (11). The tertiary colours (2, 4, 6, 8, 10 and 12 on the colour wheel) are made by mixing equal quantities of the primary and secondary colours.

It is also important to know about complementary colours, tints and shades. Complementary colours are the two colours that lie opposite each other on the colour wheel. Any two primary colours mixed together will create the complementary colour of the remaining primary colour. Therefore, mixing red (1) and blue (5) creates purple (3), which is the complementary colour of yellow (9). Mixing blue (5) and yellow (9) creates green (7), which is the complementary colour of red (1). Finally, mixing yellow (9) and red (1) creates orange (11), which is the complementary colour of blue (5).

A tint is simply a colour that is made lighter by adding white, while a shade is a colour that is darkened by adding black or dark blue. With both tints and shades, you should add colours sparingly until you achieve the result you want.

Hints on Mixing Colours

Golden-yellow: lemon yellow plus a touch of orange or red.
Lime-green: green plus some yellow.
Sea-green: green plus royal blue.
Brick-red: brown plus red.
Orange: lemon yellow plus red.
Grey: black plus white.
Tan: brown plus a little yellow.
Flesh: pink plus a little yellow.

perfect cake coverings

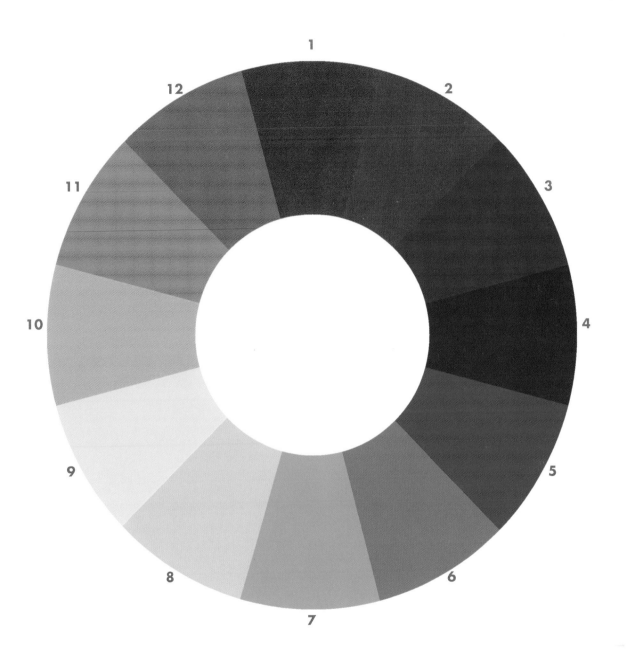

The Colour Wheel

perfect cake coverings

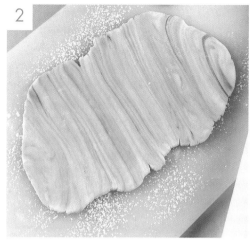

Marbling Sugarpaste

Before you begin, make sure you have the correct amount of kneaded white or ivory sugarpaste (see Sugarpaste Guide, page 110, and Kneading Sugarpaste, page 33) and a choice of paste food colouring. Follow Method One if you want a delicate marbling effect. Method Two gives a bolder, brighter result.

Method One

1. Place the sugarpaste on a surface lightly dusted with icing (confectioners') sugar and, using your hands, roll it into a sausage shape.

2. Dip the tip of a sharp knife into your chosen food colouring. Slice into the top of the sugarpaste and drag the knife, leaving a trail of food colouring. Repeat with as many colours as you like (Fig. 1).

3. Fold the sugarpaste sausage in half and roll it into a sausage shape once again. Repeat. You now have two choices. Either go for straight lines of colour, which are great for wood effects, or a swirl pattern, which always looks striking on novelty cakes.

STRAIGHT LINES

1. Twist, then roll the sugarpaste sausage as many times as you can before it starts to dry out.

2. Roll out the sugarpaste on a work surface lightly dusted with icing sugar (Fig. 2). If the sugarpaste sticks to the surface, free it by running a palette knife (metal spatula) underneath it. (The marbled effect could be spoiled if you roll up the sugarpaste and start again.) Check the underside of the sugarpaste to see which side has the best marbled effect.

SWIRLS

1. Knead the sugarpaste sausage a little, then roll it out on a surface lightly dusted

Troubleshooting

Do not be tempted to add too many colours when you are marbling sugarpaste (rolled fondant or ready-to-roll icing). The best results are often achieved using no more than three.

perfect cake coverings

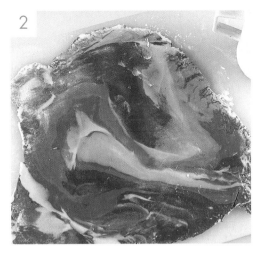

with icing sugar. The more you knead it,
the more swirled and mixed the colours
will be. Check the underside of the
sugarpaste to see which side has the
best marbled effect.

Method Two

1. Place some sugarpaste in the colour of
your choice on a surface lightly dusted with
icing (confectioners') sugar and, using your
hands, roll it into a sausage shape.

2. Roll out a thin sausage of different-
coloured sugarpaste and wrap it round the
main sausage. Repeat with as many colours
as you like (Fig. 1).

3. Roll the sugarpaste sausage on the work
surface, fold it in half, then proceed as for
Straight Lines or Swirls (Fig. 2) in Method
One, opposite.

Techniques

The purple sugarpaste (rolled fondant or
ready-to-roll icing) you end up with after
combining red and blue ready-made
sugarpaste – or red and blue food
colouring – often looks dull and dirty.
Spare yourself the disappointment by
buying ready-made purple sugarpaste.

perfect cake coverings

CHAPTER FOUR

SIMPLE DECORATING TECHNIQUES

This section takes you through a range of quick and easy decorating techniques using sugarpaste (rolled fondant or ready-to-roll icing), from cut-outs and crimping to stippling and quilling. All will give covered cakes and boards that unmistakably professional touch.

Ribbons

Ribbons make fantastic decorations, instantly transforming the simplest cakes into something special. Always use a good-quality, double-faced ribbon, which is less likely to fray than a single-faced ribbon. And before you start decorating your cake or board, set it on a turntable. This will allow you to rotate the cake or board with one hand, while you attach the ribbon with the other hand.

Attaching Ribbons to Covered Cakes

All you need to attach a ribbon to a covered cake is a little warm, previously boiled water or some royal icing (see Piping, page 66). To achieve the best results, set the ribbon in place while the covering is still damp.

1. Loosely wrap the ribbon, while it is still on the roll, round the cake to determine the length you will require.

2. Cut the ribbon to length, then wet it in a bowl of warm, previously boiled water. Run your finger down the ribbon to remove any excess water (Fig. 1). Starting at the back of the cake or at a point that will not be too visible, position the ribbon round the cake (Fig. 2). The moisture will hold it in place.

2

If you are putting a pale ribbon on a dark cake, use royal icing instead of water, which could cause the sugarpaste (rolled fondant or ready-to-roll icing) to stain the ribbon. Apply a dot of royal icing on the side of the cake (Fig. 3) and press one end of the ribbon

3

1

simple decorating techniques

against it. Wrap the ribbon round the cake and attach the other end with a few more dots of royal icing (Fig. 4). The ribbon overlap should be no more than 2.5cm (1in) to keep it looking neat.

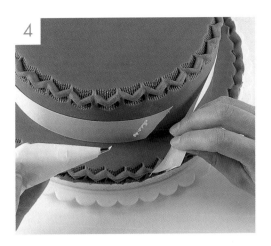

Troubleshooting

Never use pins to hold a ribbon in place on a cake. Whenever you pierce a cake, you invite bacteria to grow inside it.

Attaching Ribbons to Boards

Many people use either 12-mm ($\frac{1}{2}$-in) or 15-mm ($\frac{5}{8}$-in) ribbon to decorate boards, and stick them on with double-sided tape, glue dots or pins. It is far easier, however, to use a glue stick.

1. Loosely wrap the ribbon, while it is still on the roll, round the board to determine the length you will require.

2. Cut the ribbon to length, then go over the edges of the board with a glue stick. Carefully attach the ribbon, starting at the back of the board or at a point that will not be too visible. Apply an extra layer of glue where the ribbon overlaps (Fig. 1).

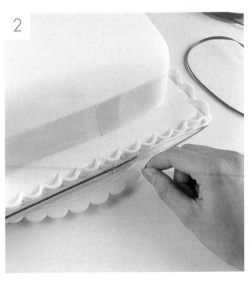

3. If you want to attach a 3-mm ($\frac{1}{8}$-in), contrasting ribbon to the wider ribbon, measure out the amount you will need and cut it to length, as in steps 1 and 2. Run the glue stick over the wider ribbon.

4. Position the 3-mm ($\frac{1}{8}$-in) ribbon in the centre of the wider ribbon, again starting at the back of the board or at a point that will not be too visible, and wrap it round the board (Fig. 2).

49

simple decorating techniques

Tying Bows

If you decide to finish off your cake or board with a bow, try to do it without introducing a twist to the ribbon, as shown opposite (Figs 1 to 4). Attach the completed bow with a few dots of royal icing (Figs 5 and 6). See page 66 for more information on piping.

Sausage Edges

The sausage edge, essentially a long, thin sugarpaste (rolled fondant or ready-to-roll icing) sausage, is the easiest cake decoration to achieve and makes a terrific finishing touch, particularly for covered novelty cakes.

1. Take a piece of kneaded sugarpaste and roll it on a work surface lightly dusted with icing (confectioners') sugar until you have a long, thin sausage. You can use your fingers, but a smoother gives you more control over the thickness of the sausage (Fig. 1).

2. Dampen round the base of the cake using a paintbrush and a little previously boiled water. Beginning at the back of the cake, or at a point that will not be too visible, start attaching the sugarpaste sausage.

3. Run the sausage all the way round the cake (Fig 2), letting the ends overlap. Using

Troubleshooting

If you accidentally get water droplets on a cake's covering, blot it off immediately with kitchen paper (paper towels), then rub a little icing (confectioners') sugar over the affected area. If you leave the water, it will create a watermark and could eat a hole in the sugarpaste (rolled fondant or ready-to-roll icing).

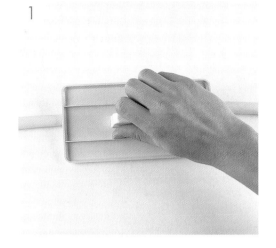

1

2

a sharp knife, cut through the overlapping pieces. Take off the top section of sugarpaste, then gently lift and remove the piece underneath it. You should find that you can butt the two ends together for a perfect join.

51

Texture

You can use nearly any tools or materials to add texture to covered boards. Just do not restrict yourself to textured mats or rolling pins, which are expensive and limited in their designs.

1. Starting in the corners of a freshly covered board (the covered cake does not need to be in position, although it is here), press down the pointed end of a Cel stick, being sure not to drag or push it so hard that you split the sugarpaste (rolled fondant or ready-to-roll icing) and expose the board beneath.

2. Repeat round the board, keeping the spaces between the impressions regular (Fig. 1). You could also use this technique to add texture to a sausage edge (see page 51).

Using Wallpaper to Create Texture

You will need a freshly covered board and a piece of heavily embossed, ideally washable wallpaper, which will not lose any fibres, for this technique.

Tools of the Trade

A sheet of plastic tile spacers, which you can find at any DIY store, gives covered cakes and boards a fantastic textured effect, resembling quilting. Cut out a section, place it against a covered board or the top or side of a covered cake and use a smoother to evenly press down the tile spacers. Repeat round the board or cake. Experiment with the size and shape of the cut-out sections to create different designs.

1

Lay the wallpaper face down on top of the covered board. Go over it with a smoother, keeping your movements as firm and even as possible, then gently peel off the wallpaper to reveal the design. Bear in mind that if you have a textured board, you will need fewer decorations on the cake itself. The old saying 'less is more' definitely applies here.

Twisted Edges

Also called ropes, these are no more than two or three sugarpaste (rolled fondant or ready-to-roll icing) sausages twisted together, then attached to covered cakes or boards. You must work quickly when you attempt this cake decoration. The longer the sugarpaste is exposed to the air, the more likely it is to split and crack – a disaster if you are trying to twist it.

simple decorating techniques

1

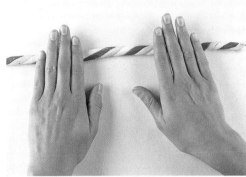

3

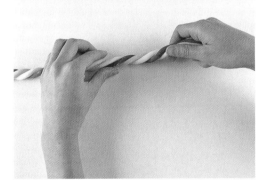

2

Techniques

You can strengthen sugarpaste (rolled fondant or ready-to-roll icing) and make it more flexible by combining half sugarpaste and half flowerpaste. Flowerpaste is an extremely pliable paste that can be rolled out so thinly, you can almost see through it.

Attaching Twisted Edges to Boards

1. Place two or three pieces of kneaded, different-coloured sugarpaste on a work surface lightly dusted with icing (confectioners') sugar and roll them until they become long, thin sausages. You can use your fingers, but a smoother gives you more control over the thickness of the sausages.

2. Using a paintbrush, dampen the sausages with a little previously boiled water, then lay them side by side (Fig. 1).

3. Very gently start twisting the sausages together (Fig. 2). Be sure not to twist them too tightly, as they are prone to splitting.

4. Continue twisting the sausages until you reach the ends, then gently roll the entire twisted edge with your fingers, so the strands hold together (Fig. 3).

5. With the paintbrush, dampen the covered board with a little previously boiled water. Beginning at the back of the board or at a point that will not be too visible, start attaching the twisted edge. (You can either

53

Troubleshooting

When you are making a twisted edge, cover each sugarpaste (rolled fondant or ready-to-roll icing) sausage with cling film (plastic wrap) as soon as you finish it. This will prevent it from drying out while you work on the other sugarpaste sausages.

do this before or after the covered cake is set in position, as it is here.) Run the twisted edge all the way round the board (Fig. 4).

6. Using a sharp knife, cut through the overlapping pieces of twisted edge. Take off the top section, then gently lift and remove the piece underneath it. You should find that you can now butt the two ends together for a perfect join.

Attaching Twisted Edges to Cakes

1. Roll out and twist three pieces of kneaded, different-coloured sugarpaste, as in Attaching Twisted Edges to Boards, steps 1 to 4 (see page 53).

2. Using a paintbrush, dampen the sides of the covered cake with dabs of previously boiled water wherever you want the twisted

edge to go. Gently attach the twisted edge, looping it up at the corners (Fig. 1).

3. Tidy up the ends of the twisted edge as in Attaching Twisted Edges to Boards, step 6, left. Cover the join with a simple twisted-edge bow (see below), if you wish.

Twisted-Edge Bows

1. Take two pieces of twisted edge (see Attaching Twisted Edges to Boards, steps 1 to 4, page 53), with one piece slightly longer than the other.

2. Pipe a little royal icing on the cake, on the end of the twisted edge (see Piping, page 66). Bend the shorter piece of twisted edge that you made in step 1 in half so it resembles the tails of a bow. Gently press it on top of the royal icing (Fig. 2).

Timesaving Tip

Make the sugarpaste (rolled fondant or ready-to-roll) sausages with a sugarcraft gun, which you can find at any sugarcraft or cook shop. Using the largest circle disk, simply squeeze the sugarpaste through it, then twist the sausages.

simple decorating techniques

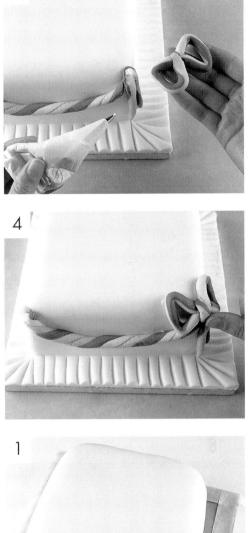

2. Using a palette knife (metal spatula), spread a thin layer of royal icing over the area that you want to stipple. Immediately begin dabbing at it with the cling film, as is used here, or the kitchen foil, scourer or sponge (Fig. 2).

3. Let the royal icing dry, then peel back the masking tape border. The stippled area should be left with crisp, clean edges (Fig. 3).

Embossing

There are all sorts of embossers available, which you can use to stamp pictures or words into freshly covered cakes or boards. There are even sets containing individual letters, so you can create any message you like. Do not forget that many household items can also double as embossers; buttons, the pointed tops of piping tubes (nozzles) and spoon handles all work well.

Spend some time practising with your embosser, so you know just how much pressure to apply when you are working on a covered cake or board. Roll out a piece of kneaded sugarpaste (rolled fondant or ready-to-roll icing), apply it to a board and experiment with the different effects you can achieve. When you are feeling confident, try simple tricks, such as sprinkling coloured food dust on a piece of kitchen paper (paper

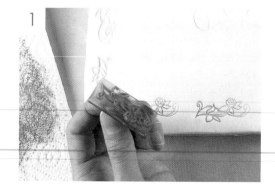

towel) and lightly rubbing the embosser in it. When you press the embosser into the sugarpaste, it will leave a coloured design, which looks quite professional (Fig. 1).

Timesaving Tip

If you are using a button as an embosser, you may find that it can be difficult to grip. Try gluing a golf tee to one side of the button. This will give you a brilliant handle and much greater control over the embosser.

Piping Embossing

You will need basic piping skills (see page 66) before you can attempt this technique, which involves piping royal icing over the designs embossed on a covered cake or board.

1. Using a plain writing tube, pipe your design onto a sheet of Perspex with royal icing (Fig. 1).

2. Wait until the royal icing has dried, then flip over the Perspex and press it into a freshly covered cake or board (Fig. 2).

3. Gently lift the Perspex, then pipe over the embossed design with royal icing (Fig. 3).

Thinking Ahead

Remember that you must always crimp freshly covered cakes. As soon as the sugarpaste (rolled fondant or ready-to-roll icing) begins to crust, it is too late. Plan your design ahead of time and have your adjusted crimper close to hand while you are covering your cake or board.

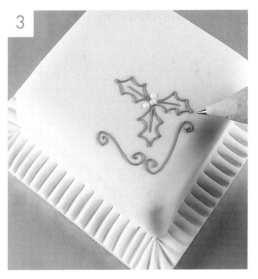

Crimping

Inexpensive and easy to use, crimpers give freshly covered cakes and boards neat, decorative edges in no time. They come in all shapes and sizes, producing everything from curved lines to diamond shapes.

Always give yourself some time to practise with your crimpers before you start working on a cake, to make sure you are applying the right amount of pressure. Roll out a piece of kneaded sugarpaste (rolled fondant or ready-to-roll icing), apply it to a board and experiment with the different effects you can achieve.

57

1. Adjust the O ring on the crimper until you are happy with the distance between the ends. The further apart the ends are, the wider your crimping will be.

2. If you are crimping onto a flat surface, hold the crimper straight. If you are using it on the edge of a cake or board, however, it is better to hold it at a 45° angle.

3. Push the crimper just a little way into the sugarpaste and squeeze the ends together to create the effect you want (Fig. 1). Do not dig the crimper too far into the sugarpaste, or you will expose the cake underneath.

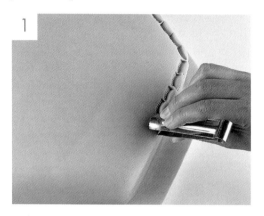

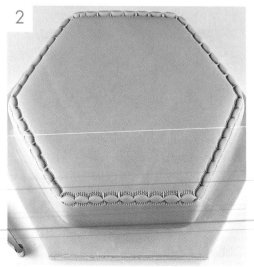

4. Gently release and lift off the crimper, making sure it does not spring apart and tear the sugarpaste.

5. Repeat steps 3 and 4 round the cake, making sure each crimp starts next to the previous one, without leaving a gap (Fig. 2).

Inner Crimping

Inner crimping (ie, crimping a design centrally on top of a cake) looks nice on large cakes that do not have much decoration on the top. It draws the eye to the middle of the cake, where you will presumably want to put any words or designs, and saves you having to think of other ways to fill the space. To keep the lines straight, place a thin board or a thick piece of paper on the top of the cake and use it as a guide. Make sure it is in the centre of the cake, so you leave a uniform amount of space all the way round it.

Cut-outs

Cut-outs always look impressive, belying the fact that they require very little effort. You will need to give your cake or board a double covering of sugarpaste (rolled fondant or ready-to-roll icing). However, after that, all that is left is to cut out shapes from the covering with a cutter, then to reattach them in an attractive pattern.

1. Cover the cake or board – or both – with a thin coating of sugarpaste and leave it to dry. This coating looks best if it is in a contrasting shade to the main sugarpaste covering that you will add in step 3.

2. Decide roughly where you will be cutting out the shapes and moisten the sugarpaste around these areas with a paintbrush and

simple decorating techniques

1

2

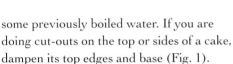

3

4

some previously boiled water. If you are doing cut-outs on the top or sides of a cake, dampen its top edges and base (Fig. 1).

3. Cover the cake or board with a normal coating of sugarpaste.

4. While the covering is still damp, cut out shapes using a cutter, making sure you leave crisp, clean edges and only cut though the top layer of sugarpaste.

5. Lift out the shapes (Fig. 2), dab them with a little previously boiled water (Fig. 3) and stick them back on the cake in any pattern you like (Fig. 4). You could also place small cut-out shapes, either cut from the covering or from another piece of rolled-out sugarpaste, on top of the larger shapes. This technique is known as overlaying.

Inserts

Also known as inlays, these are simply cut-out sugarpaste (rolled fondant or ready-to-roll icing) shapes that are left to dry, decorated and dropped into a hollow on the surface of a cake or board that has been made using the same cutter.

59

As with cut-outs (see page 58), you will need to give the cake or board a thin coating of sugarpaste (rolled fondant or ready-to-roll icing) before applying the regular covering, which should ideally be in a contrasting colour. If you would like to use an insert that is a different colour from either of these coverings, roll out a small amount of sugarpaste in the desired colour and cut out a shape that will match the hollow on the covering.

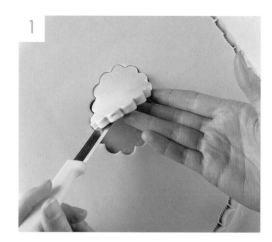

1. Cover a cake or board and cut out a shape with a cutter, as described in Cut-Outs, steps 1 to 4 (see pages 58–9).

2. Use a knife to lift out the shape if it is large (Fig. 1), then set it on a piece of foam. This will allow the air to circulate around the shape and dry all sides at once.

3. Once the shape is completely dry, decorate it any way you like. Simple piping or quilling looks nice (see Piping, page 66, and Quilling, below).

4. When the decorations have dried, pipe a little royal icing in the hollow in the covering and slip in the insert (Fig. 2).

Quilling

Most people have seen quilling or curlicues, a sort of filigree, practised with paper, but it also works beautifully with Mexican paste, a hard-drying modelling paste. See page 125 for the recipe.

1. Roll out a piece of Mexican paste until it is wafer thin.

2. Using a pizza wheel, cut the Mexican paste into several very fine strips.

3. Roll the strips round a cocktail stick (toothpick), coiling tightly at first, then allowing the coil to loosen at the end (Fig. 1).

simple decorating techniques

4. Gently remove the coils from the cocktail stick, dab them with a paintbrush and a little previously boiled water and either attach them to an insert (Fig. 2) or a covered cake or board.

Timesaving Tip

If you are painting small areas on a covered cake or board, replace the water in the food-colouring mixture with gin or vodka. Both dry very quickly.

Painting

Paintwork looks particularly nice on covered novelty cakes. Once the covering is embossed with the tin's design (see Covering Novelty Cakes, step 2, page 39), you will have clear outlines with which to work. You will need a selection of watered-down paste food colouring – do not be afraid to mix these as you would watercolour paints to achieve the shades you want – and a large paintbrush. The bigger the paintbrush, the smoother your paintwork will be.

Leave the embossed cake to dry for at least 24 hours, then gradually add details and shading with the watered-down food colouring (Fig. 1). If you make a mistake, go over it with a clean, damp paintbrush, pat the area dry with a piece of kitchen paper (paper towel) and repeat as necessary.

CHAPTER FIVE

ADVANCED DECORATING TECHNIQUES

Once you have mastered basic decorating techniques,
try your hand at frills, piping and basic modelling.
With practice, the finished results will make the
perfect focal point for any cake.

Frills

Sugarpaste (rolled fondant or ready-to-roll icing) or Mexican paste frills add real flair to covered cakes. All you need to create them is a template (see below) and a garrett frill cutter with interchangeable centres, which will allow you to create frills in a range of sizes. Always apply frills to a cake that has been covered at least 24 hours beforehand, so the sugarpaste is not marked when you attach them.

Making Side Templates

1. Measure the height and circumference of the cake with a tape measure. Then, either buy greaseproof (waxed) paper on a roll that matches the height of the cake and cut it to length, or cut a strip of greaseproof paper to the correct measurements. Wrap the greaseproof paper loosely round the cake to make sure it is the right size (Fig. 1).

2. Fold the greaseproof paper in half, then in half again and so on, forming as many sections as there are to be frills round the cake.

3. Place a rounded object halfway over the folded template and draw a line round it, from one side of the template to the other (Fig. 2).

4. Carefully cut along the line and open up the template. Attach it to the cake with a little masking tape and, using the pointed end of a Cel stick, lightly trace the outline of the template on the sugarpaste (Fig. 3).

Making Frills

1. Make a side template, attach it to a cake that has been covered at least 24 hours previously and trace the outline of the template onto the cake's covering, as described above.

Techniques

If you want to make frills stand out more, roll up small pieces of tissue paper or foam and place them under the frills after they are attached to the cake. Do not forget to remove the paper or foam once the frills have dried.

advanced decorating techniques

2. Roll out a small piece of kneaded sugarpaste or Mexican paste as thinly as you can. The piece really must be small; you will be working on a single frill at a time, and exposure to the air will dry out a larger piece long before you can use it all.

3. Insert your choice of centre into the garrett frill cutter (Fig. 1), then gently press the garrett frill cutter into the sugarpaste to cut out a frill. Remove the centre of the frill (Fig. 2).

4. Place the pointed end of a Cel stick on the outer edge of the frill. Roll the Cel stick backwards and forwards on the scalloped edges until they begin to lift. Continue all the way round the frill (Fig. 3).

5. Slice open the circle with a sharp knife, then ease it into a straight line (Fig. 4). Turn it over, so the neat side shows.

6. Using a paintbrush, dampen the design you traced onto the cake covering in step 1 with a little previously boiled water.

7. Lift the frill with the Cel stick and set it in place, turning its ends under to give a neat finish (Fig. 5). If the frill does not fit your template, simply cut out another frill, turn its ends under as above and join it to the first frill.

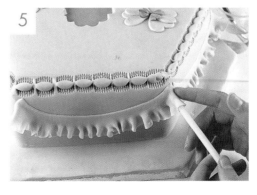

65

advanced decorating techniques

Piping

Many people regard piping as a complicated and mysterious art, but there is no better way to transform royal icing into lines, scrolls, stars or shells.

Before you begin, you will either need to buy ready-made piping (decorating) bags or make your own out of good-quality greaseproof (waxed) paper (see opposite). It makes sense to create a range of bags out of equilateral triangles – with at least one 30-cm (12-in) bag and one 20-cm (8-in) bag for more delicate piping – so you have a suitable piping bag for every job.

You will also need a selection of piping tubes (nozzles) There is a bewildering range available, but the most useful ones are the number 1, 1.5, 2 and 3 plain writing tubes and number 6, 7 and 8 shell and star tubes. Stainless steel piping tubes are better than plastic ones, because they last longer and give a crisper finish to the royal icing.

Working with Royal Icing

Royal icing is the best icing to use for piping. Made from egg whites (albumen) and icing (confectioners') sugar, it sets hard and can be used to create a range of elaborate effects. To soften its consistency, simply add a few drops of previously boiled water or a little glycerine, as in the recipe, right. The glycerine will enable you to cut cleanly through the royal icing without shattering it.

Certain piping techniques call for full-peak or soft-peak royal icing. These terms refer to the strength of the icing: when it is beaten so thoroughly that it stands in peaks when you lift your whisk out of the mixing bowl, it is full peak. Soft-peak royal icing is beaten for a shorter period, so that when you lift your whisk out of the mixing bowl, the tops of the peaks fold over. Soft-peak royal icing is ideal for covering cakes and

for fine piping work; full-peak royal icing is good for ordinary piping work.

As for piping itself: it is simply a question of pressure. When you squeeze the piping bag, the royal icing comes out; and when you stop, it does, too.

Making Royal Icing

INGREDIENTS

(see page 124 for specific amounts)
Egg whites (albumen)
Icing (confectioners') sugar
Glycerine (optional)

METHOD

1. Place the egg whites (albumen) in a bowl and beat, adding most of the icing (confectioners') sugar a spoonful at a time.

2. Add the glycerine, if used.

3. Continue beating in the icing sugar until you have achieved the right consistency.

4. Store the royal icing in an airtight container for up to a week. To get the best results, stir it once a day and then again just before use. There is no need to refrigerate royal icing.

Colouring Royal Icing

Always use paste food colouring when you are working with royal icing. Liquid food colouring softens the consistency of the icing and makes it too runny to hold its shape when it is piped.

1. Using a cocktail stick (toothpick), sparingly add some food colouring to the royal icing (Fig. 1). If you add too much colouring at one time, the royal icing will quickly become too dark.

66

advanced decorating techniques

2. Mix the royal icing with a palette knife (metal spatula) until it is evenly coloured (Fig. 2), then cover it with a damp cloth until you are ready to begin piping.

Making Piping (Decorating) Bags

1. Cut some greaseproof (waxed) paper into an equilateral triangle.

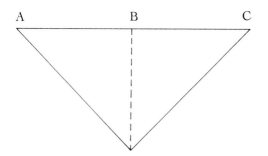

2. Pick up corner C and fold it over, so that B forms a sharp cone shape.

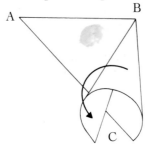

3. Wrap corner A around the cone.

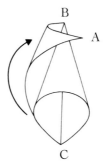

4. Make sure A and C are at the back of the cone and that the point of the cone is sharp.

5. Fold points A and C inside the top edge of the bag to hold it securely. Snip off the end of B and insert a piping tube.

advanced decorating techniques

Inserting Piping Tubes (Nozzles)

When you drop a piping tube (nozzle) into a piping (decorating) bag, approximately two-thirds of it should sit inside the bag, with one-third of it showing (Fig. 1). If any more than this shows, the piping bag may split when you start to apply pressure.

Filling Piping (Decorating) Bags

Never fill a piping (decorating) bag more than halfway with royal icing. If you overfill it, the royal icing will burst out of the piping bag, decorating everything but the cake.

1. Hold the piping bag with your thumb pressed against the seam. This will prevent it from coming undone.

2. Scoop up some royal icing with the end of a palette knife (metal spatula) and insert it into the piping bag (Fig. 1, below).

3. Squeeze the bag together at the top and gently pull out the palette knife from between the closed edges of the piping bag (Fig. 2).

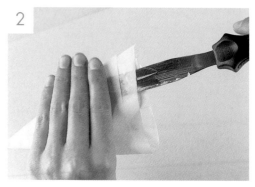

4. Fold over the top of the bag to seal it before you begin piping (Figs 3 and 4).

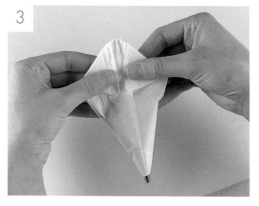

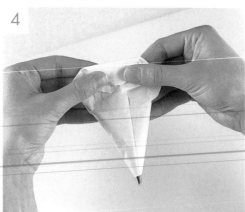

advanced decorating techniques

Simple Piping Techniques

By working with different piping tubes (nozzles), and altering the consistency of your royal icing and the amount of pressure you apply to the piping (decorating) bag, you can pipe everything from simple lines and dots to elegant scrolls.

Shells

FULL-PEAK ROYAL ICING

NUMBER 6, 7 OR 8 SHELL TUBE

Holding the piping bag at a 45° angle, position the piping tube on a covered cake or board. Squeeze the piping bag so the royal icing emerges all round the piping tube. Keep going until the shell is the size you want, then drag the piping tube along to create a tail. Gradually release the pressure on the piping bag as you drag the piping tube, then release the pressure entirely and lift the piping tube. Start the next shell at the end of the first shell's tail. Repeat as many times as necessary, keeping all of the shells the same size (Fig. 1).

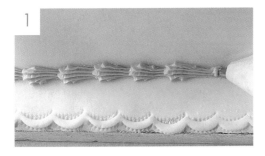

Fleurs de Lys

FULL-PEAK ROYAL ICING

NUMBER 6, 7 OR 8 SHELL TUBE

This design takes the shell method and moves it along. The first shell is piped onto a covered cake or board as described above. However, the second shell is piped just to the left of the first one, starting halfway down it and with its tail curving down towards the bottom of the first shell. The next shell is

Always use a large, 38-cm (15-in) piping (decorating) bag when you are piping shells, because they require a great deal of royal icing.

done in the same way, though it starts halfway down the right side of the second shell. Repeat as many times as necessary, keeping all of the fleurs de lys the same size (Fig. 2).

Snail Trails

SOFT-PEAK ROYAL ICING

NUMBER 1, 1.5, 2 OR 3 PLAIN WRITING TUBE

A snail trail is an excellent finishing touch for a confined area. It is formed in the same way as ordinary shells (see left); however, a plain writing tube is used. The smaller the writing tube, the more delicate the snail trail will be (Fig. 3).

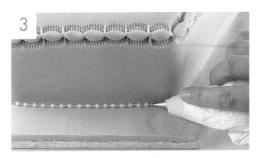

69

Bulbs

FULL-PEAK ROYAL ICING

NUMBER 1, 1.5, 2 OR 3 PLAIN WRITING TUBE

Bulbs are very easy to create, but it can take practice to get all of them the same size. The royal icing should be slightly softer than full peak, though not quite soft peak. To soften its consistency, add a little previously boiled water a drop at a time; you should not need more than two or three droplets.

Holding the piping tube vertically, position the piping tube on a covered cake or board. Squeeze the piping bag until the bulb is the size you want, then release the pressure on the

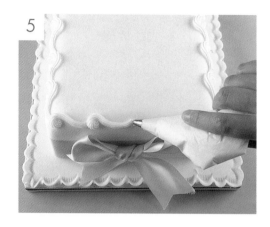

piping bag and lift the piping tube. Repeat as many times as necessary, keeping all of the bulbs the same size (Fig. 4). If you find it easier, you could also pipe the bulbs onto a plastic sleeve or wallet, which you can find at any office-supply shop. Once the bulbs are dry, pick off the best ones and position them on the cake with a little royal icing.

Troubleshooting

If the tops of your bulbs are forming little peaks, immediately brush them down with a damp paintbrush.

Scrolls

FULL-PEAK ROYAL ICING

NUMBER 6, 7 OR 8 SHELL TUBE

Holding the piping bag at a 45° angle, position the piping tube on a covered cake or board and pipe outwards in a circular movement. Return the piping tube to the cake or board, then release the pressure on the piping bag and break off the icing. Repeat, overlapping the scrolls slightly and keeping all of them the same size (Fig. 5).

Dots

SOFT-PEAK ROYAL ICING

NUMBER 1 OR 1.5 PLAIN WRITING TUBE

Piping dots is in itself quite simple, but the royal icing must be of a soft consistency so that you do not create peaks when you release the pressure on the piping bag. Experiment until you get it right (see Working with Royal Icing, page 66), then pipe the royal icing as you would bulbs, left.

Straight Lines

SOFT-PEAK ROYAL ICING

NUMBER 1, 1.5, 2 OR 3 PLAIN WRITING TUBE

Holding the piping bag vertically, position the piping tube on a covered cake or board. Lift the piping tube, at the same time applying pressure on the piping bag. Never

advanced decorating techniques

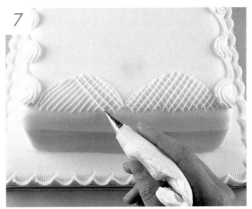

apply pressure until you are ready to start the line, and do not drag the piping tube across the cake or board. By lifting it, you will gain more control over your piping and will be able to see where you need to 'land' to finish the line. Just before you finish the line, release the pressure on the piping bag so you can complete the line in your own time.

Straight lines may not seem terribly versatile, but they can be used to create a variety of designs. The cake top in Fig. 6 features an effective line-and-dot pattern.

Trellises

SOFT-PEAK ICING

NUMBER 1, 1.5, 2 OR 3 PLAIN WRITING TUBE

This design takes straight lines to the next level. Pipe parallel lines (see Straight Lines, left) in one direction on a covered cake or board, then over-pipe lines going in the

opposite direction (Fig. 7). You can pipe a third set of lines for an even more impressive effect. The lines may be piped straight or diagonally, depending on the look you want; just try to make sure that the spacing between them is even.

Stars

FULL-PEAK ICING

NUMBER 6, 7 OR 8 STAR TUBE

Stars are formed in the exact same way as bulbs, opposite, but you will need to use a number 6, 7 or 8 star tube instead of a plain writing tube (Fig. 8).

Troubleshooting

Never use glacé icing, also known as water icing, for piping. It is too runny and will end up looking a mess.

71

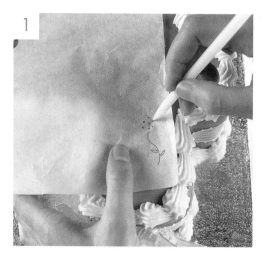

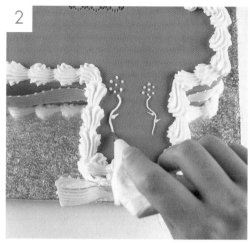

Advanced Piping Techniques

From simple piping techniques, it is a short leap to tube embroidery, pressure piping and lacework. Despite their daunting names, all three build on the royal-icing shells, bulbs, dots and lines covered on pages 69 to 71.

Tube Embroidery

Tube embroidery, as it name suggests, involves piping royal icing in the style of embroidery. All you need to do is trace or draw a pattern you like onto a piece of greaseproof (waxed) paper, then tranfer this design onto a covered cake or board using the pointed end of a Cel stick.

1. Set the piece of greaseproof paper in position on the covered cake or board and, using the pointed end of a Cel stick, mark the general outline of the design on the sugarpaste (rolled fondant or ready-to-roll icing) (Fig. 1).

2. Only put a small amount of royal icing in your piping (decorating) bag (see Filling Piping Bags, page 68); this will make the piping bag easier to hold and will give you greater freedom of movement.

3. Begin piping, holding the piping bag like a pen and allowing the piping tube (nozzle) to graze the covering of the cake or board (Fig. 2). If you make a mistake, remove it with a damp paintbrush and pipe the pattern again.

Pressure Piping

Also known as figure piping, this is an incredibly simple means of creating royal icing shapes and figures. Simply hold your piping (decorating) bag at a 90° angle, keep the piping tube (nozzle) still, then squeeze the bag until the royal icing forms a round bulb shape around the piping tube. (You can also gradually move the piping tube sideways to create an elongated shape.) Repeat as many times as necessary to build up your design.

To save time as you work, make up at least three piping bags (see page 67) beforehand, with number 1, 2 and 3 plain writing tubes. Make sure the royal icing is of a soft consistency but at the same time able to hold its shape, like whipped cream. To alter its consistency, add previously boiled water a drop at a time; you should not need more than two or three droplets. Allow each stage of your piping to dry before you begin the next stage, and add any coloured detailing at the end.

advanced decorating techniques

BABY BOOTIES

1. Using a number 2 plain writing tube, pipe a large bulb, dragging the piping tube slightly to create an elongated shape. Let the royal icing dry.

2. Pipe another, smaller bulb on one end of the bulb created in step 1. Leave it to dry.

RABBIT (BACK VIEW)

1. Using a number 2 plain writing tube, pipe a large bulb, dragging the piping tube slightly to create an elongated shape. This is the body.

2. When the first bulb has dried, pipe a small bulb at its base for the tail and another small bulb on top for the head. Leave these to dry.

3. Using a number 1 plain writing tube, pipe some royal icing round the top of the baby bootie, circling it three times. Once this has dried, use the same piping tube but a contrasting colour of royal icing (see page 66) and circle the top of the baby bootie once.

4. Finish the baby bootie with a piped bow at the front. Repeat steps 1 to 4 if you would like a pair of baby booties (Fig. 1).

3. To finish, switch to a number 1 plain writing tube to pipe two small shells (see page 69) on the head for the ears (Fig. 2).

advanced decorating techniques

3

TEDDY BEAR

1. Using a number 1 plain writing tube, pipe two small bulbs, dragging the piping tube slightly to create elongated shapes. These are the legs.

2. Once the legs have dried, switch to a number 2 plain writing tube and pipe a large bulb just above them for the body. Leave it to dry.

3. Using the number 1 plain writing tube, pipe two small bulbs for the ears and two more small, elongated bulbs for the arms.

4. Once the arms and ears have dried, use the number 2 plain writing tube to pipe a large bulb on top of the body, for the head. Let it dry.

5. Pipe a small bulb onto the head for the snout. If you like, you could pipe the nose and a bow tie using contrasting colours of

royal icing (see page 66) and a number 6 or 7 star tube. Paint on the eyes and mouth with some watered-down paste food colouring (see Painting, page 61) (Fig. 3).

BIRD

1. Using a number 2 plain writing tube, pipe a large bulb, dragging it slightly to the side to create an elongated shape. This is the body and tail.

2. Brush out the tail with a damp paintbrush, then leave it to dry.

3. Pipe a small bulb at the top of the first, large bulb (see step 1) for the head. Again, leave it to dry.

advanced decorating techniques

4. Switching to a number 1 plain writing tube, pipe a tiny bulb on the head for the beak and let it dry.

5. Pipe another small bulb onto a piece of cling film (plastic wrap) for the wing. Feather the end using the damp paintbrush.

6. Once the wing has dried, attach it to the body with a dot of royal icing. If you like, pipe a tiny bulb on the head for the eye (Fig. 4).

CATERPILLAR

1. Using a number 1 plain writing tube, pipe a snail trail (see page 69) comprising six slightly enlongated bulbs for the body. Leave it to dry.

2. Pipe a small bulb at one end of the snail trail. Let it dry, then top it with another, larger bulb for the head.

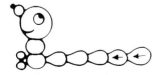

3. Once this has dried, pipe two tiny bulbs on the front of the snail trail for the legs, and another on the head, for the nose. Finish by painting on an eye and the mouth with some watered-down paste food colouring (see Painting, page 61) (Fig. 5).

DOG

1. Using a number 2 plain writing tube, pipe a large bulb, dragging the piping tube slightly to create an elongated shape. This is the body. Leave it to dry.

2. Pipe a smaller, elongated bulb opposite the one created in step 1 for the snout. The two bulbs should join up in the middle.

3. Once the body and snout are dry, pipe a large bulb just above the point where they join. This is the head. Leave it to dry.

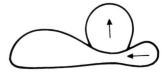

advanced decorating techniques

4. Switch to a number 1 plain writing tube and pipe two small, elongated bulbs for the front and back legs.

5. Finish by piping, in a contrasting colour of royal icing (see page 66), a tiny bulb for the nose, a small, elongated bulb for the ear and another small, elongated bulb for the tail, which can curl inwards or outwards (Fig. 6).

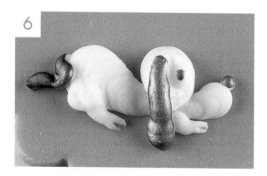

6

Lace Work

Piped lace work makes the ideal edging for covered cakes or boards. It looks fragile, but when it is made correctly, it is robust and can easily survive being transported. Just make sure your royal icing recipe does not contain glycerine, which prevents it from setting too hard (see recipe, page 66).

Before you begin, you will need to create a template and transfer it to a cake covered at least 24 hours previously (see Making Side Templates, page 64). Go through your lace collection to find a pattern you like, then trace or draw it onto a piece of plain paper. If the pattern is small, it makes sense to repeat it several times on the paper, so that once you start piping, you can continue without any interruptions.

Place the paper inside a plastic sleeve or wallet, which you can find at any office-supply shop, and secure it to a firm surface with masking tape. You will be piping directly over the design and do not want it to slip or shift. Coat the plastic sleeve with a thin layer of vegetable fat (shortening). This will prevent the lace work from sticking and breaking when you try to lift it.

1. Using a plain writing tube, pipe over the design. Keep the piping tube (nozzle) close to the surface of the plastic sleeve and try to keep the pressure even (Fig. 1).

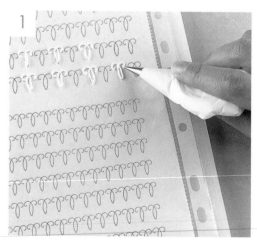

1

2. All of the lines of 'lace' should touch to prevent your work from falling apart when you lift it. Pipe more pieces than you actually need in case of any mishaps.

advanced decorating techniques

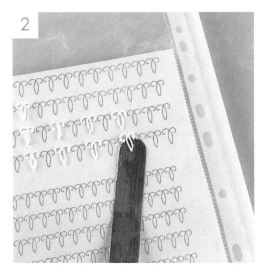

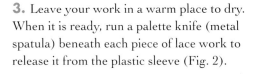

3. Leave your work in a warm place to dry. When it is ready, run a palette knife (metal spatula) beneath each piece of lace work to release it from the plastic sleeve (Fig. 2).

4. To attach the lace work to the cake, pipe a small, neat snail trail of royal icing (see page 69) along the outline that you traced on the cake or board's covering (see Making Side Templates, page 64) (Fig. 3). Alternatively, pipe two tiny dots where each piece of lace work is to be placed, and gently push the pieces on top of the dots (Fig. 4). If you use this technique, make sure that the pairs of dots are evenly spaced.

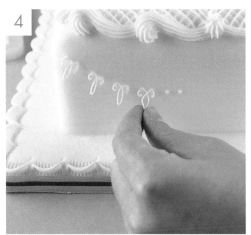

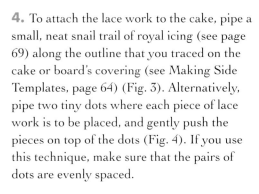

advanced decorating techniques

Special Effects

With a few tricks, sugarpaste (rolled fondant or ready-to-roll icing), food colouring, piping gel and some of the most common household ingredients can be transformed into realistic trees, grass, sand and water. Always apply special effects to a cake or board that has been covered at least 24 hours beforehand, so the covering is not marked when you set them in place.

Smooth Grass

Much less fiddly to create than ordinary grass (see right), this requires only green sugarpaste and a clean scourer. Roll out the sugarpaste into the shape you need and dab the underside with a paintbrush dampened with a little previously boiled water. Set the grass in place on a covered cake or board, then go over it with the scourer to create what appear to be strands of grass (Fig. 1).

Bushes and Grass

1. Take a lump of green sugarpaste, add a little vegetable fat (shortening) and knead the two together on a clean work surface.

2. Push the sugarpaste through a sieve (strainer), keeping the strands short for grass but making them longer for bushes.

3. With a sharp knife, cut the strands from the sieve. Dab their undersides with a paintbrush dampened with a little previously boiled water and set them in place on a covered cake or board (Fig. 2).

Water

This is one of the easiest special effects to achieve. All you need is some piping gel and paste food colouring.

1. Mix up the piping gel if you want the water to appear smooth, or leave it as it is if you prefer the look of rough, choppy water.

2. Stir food colouring into the piping gel. Then, using a palette knife (metal spatula), spread it onto a covered cake or board (Fig. 1).

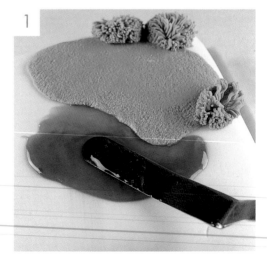

advanced decorating techniques

Techniques

Make rough water even more realistic by piping royal icing onto the crests of the waves, using a piping (decorating) bag without a piping tube (nozzle). With a paintbrush, swirl up the royal icing to create white horses.

Pebbles and Rocks

1. Take a lump of white or ivory sugarpaste and, using a cocktail stick (toothpick), add some black and brown paste food colouring.

2. Lightly knead the sugarpaste on a clean work surface, then pinch off small pieces to make uneven rocks. Roll the rocks in the palms of your hands to create pebbles.

3. Using a paintbrush, dab the undersides of the rocks and pebbles with a little previously boiled water and set them in place on a covered cake or board (Fig. 1, below).

1

2

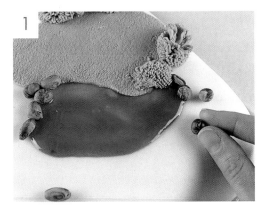

1

Fir Tree

1. Pinch off a piece of green sugarpaste and roll it into a ball. While you are still rolling it, gently apply pressure to one side of the ball with your fingers until it forms a cone shape.

2. Insert a Cel stick into the base of the cone to hold it in position. Then, using a pair of scissors, snip away at the cone until you have created some branches (Fig. 1, above).

3. Lift the tree off the Cel stick. Dab its underside with a paintbrush dampened with a little previously boiled water and set it in place on a covered cake or board (Fig. 2).

Techniques

To create lifelike sugarpaste (rolled fondant or ready-to-roll icing) grass or bushes, knead different shades of green food colouring into the sugarpaste for each plant.

Log

For this special effect, you will need gum tragacanth, a natural thickening agent. If you cannot find it, Tylo powder, its man-made equivalent, will also do.

1. Take a lump of brown sugarpaste and knead in 5ml (1 tsp) of gum tragacanth or Tylo powder for every 250g (9oz) of sugarpaste. Using your fingers, roll the sugarpaste into a cylindrical shape.

2. Hollow out the ends of the cylinder with your fingers and pull up little bits of sugarpaste all over to represent sawn-off branches (Fig. 1).

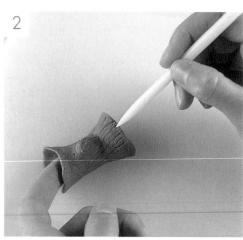

3. With the pointed end of a Cel stick, cut slits and crazing into the sugarpaste (Fig. 2).

4. Leave the sugarpaste to dry, then 'finger' the edges of the slits until they crack.

5. Using a paintbrush dampened with a little previously boiled water, dab the underside of the log and set it in place on a covered cake or board (Fig. 3).

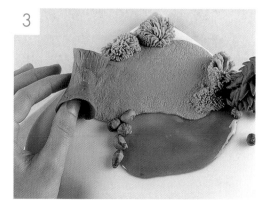

Bulrushes

This special effect calls for pieces of uncooked spaghetti, which are used to represent the bulrushes' stems. Do not be tempted to use cocktail sticks (toothpicks) or plastic supports instead, because they can be harmful if eaten.

1. Pinch off a piece of brown sugarpaste and mould it round a piece of uncooked spaghetti. Leave a little piece of spaghetti protruding at the top (Fig. 1).

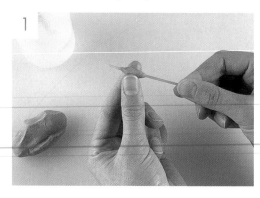

advanced decorating techniques

covered cake or board with a little previously boiled water, then sprinkle the area with the sugar mixture. Be careful not to wet the cake too much, or the sugar will dissolve.

Method Two

Take a lump of yellow sugarpaste and push it through a sieve (strainer). Leave the pieces to dry overnight in a warm, dry place; an airing cupboard is ideal. Once the sugarpaste pieces are dry, rub them between your fingers until they become fine grains (Fig. 1). Using a paintbrush, dampen the covered cake or board with a little previously boiled water, then sprinkle the area with the grains. Use a dry paintbrush to spread them evenly (Fig. 2).

2. Blend some sugar or semolina with brown food dust. Dampen the sugarpaste on the piece of spaghetti with a paintbrush and some previously boiled water, then dip it into the sugar mixture (Fig. 2).

3. Make as many bulrushes as you think you need, then press them into the covered cake or board (Fig. 3).

Sand

There are two methods for creating realistic sand. Follow the first method, which uses coloured food dust and sugar or semolina, if you need to decorate your cake quickly.

Method One

Mix some sugar with some yellow or brown food dust. Using a paintbrush, dampen a

Mud

Follow Method Two for sand, above, replacing the yellow sugarpaste with brown.

advanced decorating techniques

Bark

For this special effect, you will need gum tragacanth, a natural thickening agent. If you cannot find it, Tylo powder, its man-made equivalent, will also do.

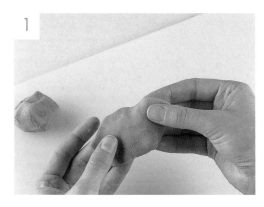

1. Take a lump of brown sugarpaste and knead in 5ml (1 tsp) of gum tragacanth or Tylo powder for every 250g (9oz) of sugarpaste. Using your fingers, roll the sugarpaste into a cylindrical shape.

2. 'Finger' the sugarpaste, flattening it and then creating lots of lumps and bumps, and a turned-up edge on one side (Fig. 1).

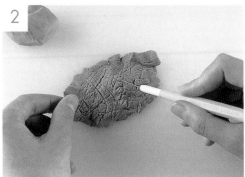

3. Using a scriber, thoroughly score the sugarpaste in all directions (Fig. 2).

4. Leave the sugarpaste to dry for half an hour, then lift and flex it, to create slits and crazing.

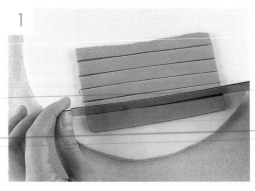

5. Set aside the sugarpaste to dry completely, then, with a paintbrush, dust it all over with brown, chestnut and green food dust, to give the bark an aged look and to create a realistic moss effect (Fig. 3). Using a clean paintbrush, dampen the underside with some previously boiled water and set the bark in place on a covered cake or board.

Bricks

1. Roll out some brown sugarpaste into the shape that you need. Using a paintbrush, dampen the underside with a little previously boiled water and set the sugarpaste in place on a covered cake or board.

2. With an icing ruler, or something of a similar thickness, mark evenly spaced horizontal lines on the sugarpaste (Fig. 1).

advanced decorating techniques

2

3

3. Cut the sausage into small segments, then roughly shape each stone into a flattened ball with your fingers.

4. Set the stones in place on the buttercream or royal icing, leaving a small gap round them so the royal icing shows through, as mortar would through real stonework (Fig. 2).

Techniques

For large stones, make the sausage in Stonework, step 2 (see left) quite thick. For smaller stones, instead make it thinner.

1

3. Mark the vertical lines, making alternate rows of bricks identical.

4. Leave the sugarpaste to dry, then pipe over the lines you made in steps 2 and 3 with a number 1 plain writing tube and some white royal icing (Fig. 2).

5. Dampen your finger with a little previously boiled water, then run it over the royal icing to press it into the lines, creating a mortar effect (Fig. 3).

Stonework

1. Using a palette knife (metal spatula), give the cake or board a thick coating of white buttercream or royal icing (Fig. 1).

2. Pinch off a piece of grey sugarpaste and roll it into a thin sausage with your fingers.

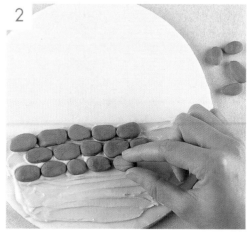

2

advanced decorating techniques

Modelling

Marzipan, sugarpaste (rolled fondant or ready-to-roll icing) and Mexican paste are the ideal mediums for modelling, because they are pliable and can be moulded into a range of shapes. Which one you use depends on the shape that you plan to model and whether or not it will be eaten.

Provided the cake's recipient does not suffer from a nut allergy, marzipan is probably the best medium. Just remember that food colouring never looks as bright when it is mixed into marzipan as it does when mixed into sugarpaste and Mexican

paste. If you are modelling shapes that require some finesse, however, Mexican paste and sugarpaste blended with gum tragacanth or Tylo powder (both are thickening agents) are preferable. As a general rule, mix 5ml (1 tsp) of gum tragacanth or Tylo powder with every 250g (9oz) of sugarpaste.

No matter what medium you use, stick together your modelled figures with sugar glue, an edible glue made from sugar, or a little warm, previously boiled water. Always give your figures plenty of time to dry; there is nothing more upsetting than having a limb drop off because you have rushed the job. Finally, try not to be intimidated by the apparent complexity of modelled figures. If you break them down, you will see that nearly all are formed from three simple shapes: a ball, a cone and a cylinder.

Ball

Take a piece of sugarpaste, marzipan or Mexican paste and, cupping the ball in your palms, roll it until it has formed a perfect sphere (Fig. 1).

Cone

Starting with a ball of sugarpaste, marzipan or Mexican paste (see above), roll it in the palms of your hands, then gently add pressure with the fingers of one hand until it has formed a cone (Fig. 2).

Cylinder

Place a ball of sugarpaste, marzipan or Mexican paste (see above) on a clean work surface. Using a smoother, roll the ball until it forms a cylinder. Slice off the ends with a sharp knife, then continue to roll the cylinder with your fingers until it is the size you want (Fig. 3).

advanced decorating techniques

Modelled Figures

Modelled figures give you the opportunity to create individual characters with a range of expressions and idiosyncracies. Do not be afraid to add quirky touches, such as the clown's jaunty hat (see page 94).

Plan ahead, making sure you have plenty of sugar glue or warm, previously boiled water to stick the modelled figures together, and enough sugarpaste, marzipan or Mexican paste in the right colours. (The colours used here are only suggestions.) In some instances, finishing touches are added with piped royal icing or food colouring, so it makes sense to have these, plus piping (decorating) bags, piping tubes (nozzles) and paintbrushes, to hand as well.

Beach Balls

1. Make two balls (see opposite) of the same size out of two different colours of sugarpaste, marzipan or Mexican paste.

2. Using a sharp knife, cut the balls in half without distorting the shapes too much. Cut these pieces in half again (Fig. 1).

3. Take two quarters of each colour and piece together a beach ball, alternating the colours (Fig. 2). Repeat with the remaining quarters to create another beach ball.

4. Finish by re-rolling the beach balls in the palms of your hands, so they hold their shapes (Fig. 3).

Duck

1. Starting with a large ball (see opposite) of sugarpaste, marzipan or Mexican paste, 'cone' it slightly by rolling it in the palms of your hands, then gently adding pressure on one end with the fingers of one hand. This is the duck's body.

2. Flatten the pointed end with your fingers to make the back tail. Using a sharp knife, mark some lines on it for the feathers.

3. Make some legs by rolling out a thin sausage of sugarpaste, marzipan or Mexican

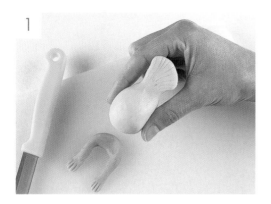

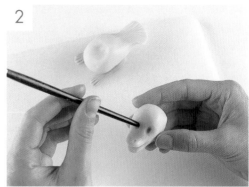

paste and flattening each end with your fingers. Using the knife, mark the ends to create webs, then bend the sausage into a U shape.

4. Dab the underside of the body with a paintbrush dampened with a little sugar glue or warm, previously boiled water and set it on top of the legs (Fig. 1).

5. Using half the amount of sugarpaste, marzipan or Mexican paste that you used to create the body, make another ball for the duck's head. 'Cone' it slightly, as described in step 1.

6. Round off the pointed end of the cone with your fingers, then, using the knife, slice open the beak. With the pointed end of a Cel stick, make two holes just above the beak for the nostrils.

7. Create two eye sockets with the end of a paintbrush handle (Fig. 2), then attach the head to the body, again using some sugar glue or water.

8. Form two medium cones (see page 84) out of sugarpaste, marzipan or Mexican paste and flatten them with your fingers to make the wings. Using the knife, mark

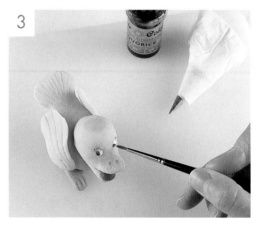

lines on them for the feathers, then attach the wings to the body with the sugar glue or water.

9. Make one more small cone for the tongue, flatten it with your fingers and place it in the mouth with the sugar glue or water. Finish by piping some royal icing into the eye sockets. Once it is dry, paint on the pupils and some eyelashes with paste food colouring (Fig. 3).

Dog
1. Make a 10-cm (4-in) long cylinder (see page 84) out of sugarpaste, marzipan or Mexican paste for the body. If you are making a dalmatian, add small, brown or black flattened balls, again out of sugarpaste,

advanced decorating techniques

marzipan or Mexican paste, to the cylinder (Fig. 1), then roll it again.

2. Slice approximately 2.5cm (1in) into one end of the cylinder with a sharp knife. Separate the two pieces and round off the ends with your fingers. Repeat on the other end of the cylinder (Fig. 2).

3. Bend the cylinder into a U shape and leave it to dry.

4. Form a medium ball (see page 84) out of sugarpaste, marzipan or Mexican paste for the head, again adding brown or black dots at this stage if you are making a dalmatian. 'Cone' the ball slightly by rolling it in the palms of your hands, then gently adding pressure on one end with the fingers of one hand.

5. Round off the pointed end of the cone with your fingers, then, with the knife, slice it open to create the mouth. Using the end of a paintbrush handle, make two holes just above the mouth for the nostrils.

6. Create two eye sockets with the end of the paintbrush handle. Then, using a paintbrush dampened with a little sugar glue or warm, previously boiled water, attach the head to the body and leave both to dry.

7. Pipe some royal icing into the eye sockets. Once it is dry, paint on the pupils and some eyelashes with paste food colouring.

8. Make a ball for the nose and four small cones (see page 84): two for the ears, one for the tongue and a thinner one for the tail. Flatten the ball and all of the cones except for the tail, then attach them to the head and body with the sugar glue or water (Fig. 3).

Teddy Bear
1. Make a large ball (see page 84) out of sugarpaste, marzipan or Mexican paste for the body.

2. Form four medium cylinders (page 84) out of sugarpaste, marzipan or Mexican paste: two for the arms and two for the legs

Gently press on the ends of the legs with your fingers to create the feet (Fig. 1).

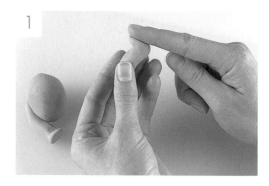

3. Using the wide end of a piping tube (nozzle), cut four small disks out of sugarpaste, marzipan or Mexican paste to make the pads for the paws. Using a paintbrush, dab their undersides with a little sugar glue or warm, previously boiled water and set them in place on the arms and legs. Attach the arms and legs to the body in the same way (Fig. 2).

4. Using half the amount of sugarpaste, marzipan or Mexican paste that you used to create the body, make another ball for the head. Hollow out the eye sockets using the end of a paintbrush handle, then attach the head to the body with the sugar glue or water and leave both to dry.

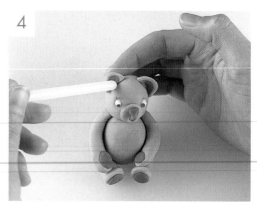

5. Pipe some royal icing into the eye sockets. Once it is dry, paint on the pupils and some eyelashes with paste food colouring.

6. Make a small, flattened ball for the snout. Repeat with a smaller, flattened ball for the nose and attach this to the first ball with the sugar glue or water. Attach the snout to the face, then use a drinking straw with half of one end cut away to create the mouth (Fig. 3).

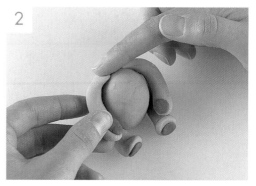

7. For the ears, make a small, flattened ball out of sugarpaste, marzipan or Mexican paste. Cut it in half with a sharp knife, trying not to distort the shape, then repeat with a slightly smaller, flattened ball.

8. Attach the smaller halves to the larger ones with the sugar glue or water, then attach the ears to the head in the same way. Curve the ears by moulding them round the blunt end of a Cel stick (Fig. 4).

advanced decorating techniques

1

2

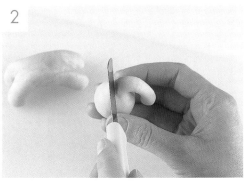

3

4. Hollow out the eye sockets with the blunt end of a Cel stick, then create another hollow on the end of the trunk in the same way.

5. Make two small, flattened balls (see page 84) out of sugarpaste, marzipan or Mexican paste for the ears. Slightly elongate them with your fingers, then set them aside.

6. Form three small cones out of sugarpaste, marzipan or Mexican paste: one for the tail, and two for the tusks. Using a paintbrush, dampen the undersides of the tusks with a little sugar glue or warm, previously boiled water and attach them to the head (Fig. 3). Attach the ears in the same way.

7. Dampen the underside of the head with the sugar glue or water and attach it to the body. Flatten one end of the tail with your fingers, use the knife to mark it with a few vertical lines, then attach it to the body in the same way (Fig. 4).

Elephant

1. Make a 10-cm (4-in) long cylinder (see page 84) out of sugarpaste, marzipan or Mexican paste for the body. Slice approximately 2.5cm (1in) into one end of the cylinder with a sharp knife. Separate the two pieces and round off the ends with your fingers. Repeat on the other end of the cylinder.

2. Bend the cylinder into a U shape and leave it to dry.

3. Form a cone (see page 84) out of sugarpaste, marzipan or Mexican paste for the head, continuing to roll one end until it has developed a trunk (Fig. 1). Using the knife, carve a few horizontal lines on the top of the trunk, which will make it easier for you to curl it upwards. Still using the knife, slice open the mouth just beneath the trunk (Fig. 2).

4

advanced decorating techniques

8. Finish by piping some royal icing into the eye sockets. Once it is dry, paint on the pupils and some eyelashes with paste food colouring.

Choirboy

1. Make a 5-cm (2-in) cone (see page 84) out of sugarpaste, marzipan or Mexican paste for the body, then, using a sharp knife, slice off the pointed end. Leave it to dry for 24 hours, so it does not collapse when the clothes are added later.

2. Using a garrett frill cutter with no centre inserted, cut two frills out of two different colours of sugarpaste, marzipan or modelling paste. Lift the scalloped edges of both frills by rolling the pointed end of a Cel stick or the end of a paintbrush handle backwards and forwards across them.

3. Mark an X in the centre of one frill with the knife (Fig. 1). Using a paintbrush, dab a little sugar glue or warm, previously boiled water on the top and sides of the body, then drape the frill over it (Fig. 2). Drape the remaining frill over the first frill (Fig. 3).

4. Make the arms by rolling a small cylinder (see page 84) out of sugarpaste, marzipan or Mexican paste and bending it into a U shape. Slice off the ends with the knife then, using the pointed end of a Cel stick, make a hole in each end of the cylinder, where the hands will be attached later. Attach the arms to the top of the body with the sugar glue or water (Fig. 4).

5. Using the medium-sized centre of the garrett frill cutter, cut two disks from the sugarpaste, marzipan or Mexican paste. 'Frill' them as described in step 2, then set them in place on top of the arms with the sugar glue or water.

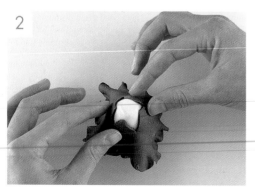

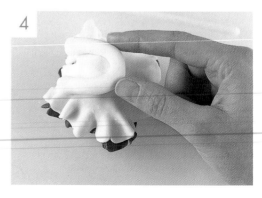

advanced decorating techniques

6. Use the garrett frill cutter's smallest centre to cut two more disks out of sugarpaste, marzipan or Mexican paste. 'Frill' them, then attach one frill to the end of each arm with the sugar glue or water. Make a hole in the centre of each frill with the pointed end of the Cel stick (Fig. 5), where the hands will be attached later.

7. Make two small cones out of sugarpaste, marzipan or Mexican paste for the hands. Flatten the wider ends with your fingers, then use the knife to mark the fingers. Dab sugar glue or water on the pointed ends of the hands and insert them into the holes you made in the frills in step 6.

8. Using half the amount of sugarpaste, marzipan or Mexican paste that you used for the body, make a small ball (see page 84) for the head. Using the end of a paintbrush handle, hollow out the mouth and the eye sockets.

9. Make a tiny ball out of sugarpaste, marzipan or Mexican paste for the nose. Mark the nostrils with the pointed end of the Cel stick, then attach the nose to the head with the sugar glue or water.

10. Attach the head to the body in the same way and leave both to dry.

11. Pipe some royal icing into the eye sockets. Once it has dried, paint on the pupils with paste food colouring. You could also water down some paste food colouring and paint the cheeks and the inside of the mouth.

12. Finish by pressing some sugarpaste, marzipan or Mexican paste through a sieve (strainer) to create strands of hair. Dampen the head with the sugar glue or water and attach the hair (Fig. 6).

Thinking Ahead

Modelled figures need to dry before you can position them on a covered cake or board. Rest them on a piece of foam, which will allow the air to circulate and dry all sides at the same time, and put this in a warm, dry place, such as an empty airing cupboard.

Alternatively, leave the shapes on a bed of cornflour (cornstarch), which will absorb any moisture, for about 24 hours. The only downside to this method is that the modelled shapes will be coated in the cornflour when you remove them. Simply dust them with a clean, dry paintbrush, and the cornflour will fall away.

5

6

advanced decorating techniques

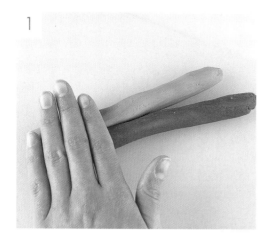

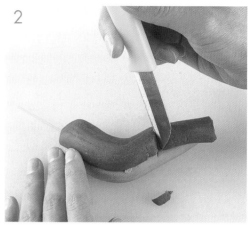

Clown

1. Make two cylinders (see page 84) of the same size out of two different colours of sugarpaste, marzipan or Mexican paste. Lay them side by side. Dab the top half of each cylinder with a paintbrush dampened with a little sugar glue or warm, previously boiled water, and roll the top halves together. This is the midsection and legs (Fig. 1).

2. Slice off the top of the midsection and the bottom of the legs with a sharp knife, then manipulate the midsection into a sitting position. Insert a piece of uncooked spaghetti through the midsection to give it some extra support.

3. With the knife, slice a V halfway down one of the legs, which will make it easier for you to bend it (Fig. 2). (This technique also works with arms.) Using the pointed end of a Cel stick, make a hollow at the end of each leg, where the shoes will be attached later.

4. Form two more cylinders out of two different colours of sugarpaste, marzipan or Mexican paste – this time making both of them narrower at one end – for the arms. Slice off the ends with the knife, then use the

pointed end of the Cel stick to hollow out one end of each arm (Fig. 3). The hands will be attached here later.

5. Attach the arms to the body with the sugar glue or water, ideally pairing an arm of one colour with a contrasting colour on the midsection.

6. Using the medium-sized centre of a garrett frill cutter, cut out two disks of two different colours from the sugarpaste, marzipan or Mexican paste. Lift the edges of both disks by rolling the pointed end of a Cel stick or the end of a paintbrush handle

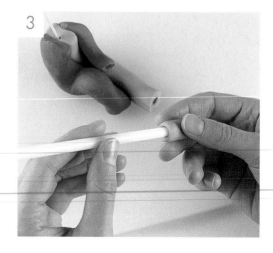

advanced decorating techniques

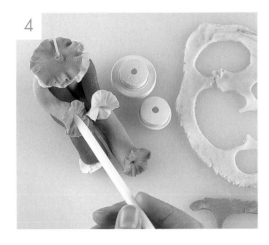

4

backwards and forwards across them. Slide the frills down the piece of spaghetti so they rest on top of the body.

7. Use the smallest centre of the garrett frill cutter to cut out four more disks: two in one colour of sugarpaste, marzipan or Mexican paste, and two in another colour. 'Frill' them as described in step 6, then attach one each to the arms and legs with the sugar glue or water. Ideally, you should have a frill of each colour on the arms, and the same for the legs.

8. Using the pointed end of the Cel stick, make a hole in the centre of each frill (Fig. 4), where the hands and shoes will be attached later.

9. Make two small cones (see page 84) out of sugarpaste, marzipan or Mexican paste for the hands, flatten the wider ends with your fingers, then use the sharp knife to mark the fingers. You could also add some fingernails with a drinking straw, with half of one end cut away. Dab the pointed ends of the hands with the sugar glue or water, then insert them into the frills on the arms.

10. Make a ball (see page 84) out of sugarpaste, marzipan or Mexican paste for the head. Using the pointed end of the Cel stick, make two small holes for the eyes. Use the drinking straw to make the mouth. Form a tiny ball out of sugarpaste, marzipan or Mexican paste for the nose and attach it to the face with the sugar glue or water.

11. Dab the sugar glue or water on the bottom of the head, then slide it down the piece of spaghetti until it rests on top of the body. Do not worry if the spaghetti protrudes from the top of the head; you can either use it to secure a hat or snap it off just before you add the hair later.

12. Using a paintbrush and some watered-down paste food colouring, paint the clown's cheeks and mouth, and some X marks over the eyes.

13. Make two small cylinders out of sugarpaste, marzipan or Mexican paste for the shoes and mould one end of each cylinder into a point with your fingers. Use the blunt end of the knife to flatten out the soles of the shoes and to create heels (Fig. 5). Pinch up the centre of each cylinder into a point,

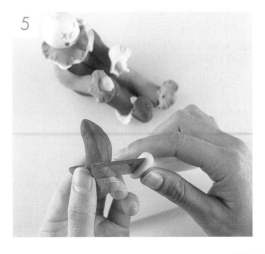

5

93

6

dab it with the sugar glue or water, and insert it into the frills on the legs. Add two tiny balls made out of sugarpaste, marzipan or Mexican paste to the tips of the shoes, to represent pom-poms.

14. Finish by pressing some sugarpaste, marzipan or Mexican paste through a sieve (strainer) to create strands of hair. Dampen the head with the sugar glue or water, and attach the hair. You could also add a hat (formed from a cone and decorated with tiny balls for pom-poms), if you like (Fig. 6).

Comic Figures

Caricatures of friends and loved ones are often easier to achieve than faithful representations – and they are always sure to raise a smile.

Troubleshooting

The clown and comic figures can be made in any size; however, just remember that the larger they are, the heftier their legs and bodies must be. Roll thicker cylinders and cones accordingly.

GENTLEMAN

1. Make a long cylinder (see page 84) out of sugarpaste, marzipan or Mexican paste for the trouser legs. Bend it in half, then use a sharp knife to slice off the top and bottom ends (Fig. 1).

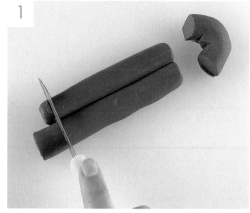

1

Tools of the Trade

Pieces of uncooked spaghetti create ideal supports for modelled figures, because they will not harm anyone if they are eaten. For this reason, avoid using cocktail sticks (toothpicks) or plastic supports. If you really must use these, put a warning on the cake, stating that the modelled figure is an inedible decoration.

2. Using a paintbrush, dampen the cylinders with a little sugar glue or warm, previously boiled water and stick them together. Press a piece of uncooked spaghetti down one trouser leg to give it extra support.

3. Using the pointed end of a Cel stick, make two hollows at the ends of the trouser legs, for the shoes.

advanced decorating techniques

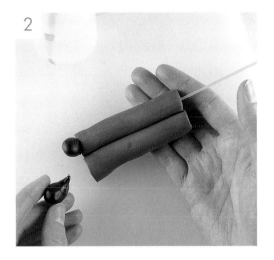

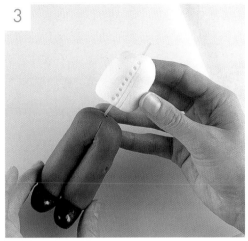

4. Form two small cylinders out of sugarpaste, marzipan or Mexican paste for the shoes. Round one end of each shoe with your fingers, and pinch up the other end. Dab the pointed ends of the shoes with the sugar glue or water and insert them into the trouser legs (Fig. 2).

5. Once the shoes have dried, coat them with confectionery glaze, which is available at any sugarcraft or cook shop, to make them shine.

6. Make another cylinder out of sugarpaste, marzipan or Mexican paste for the midsection and 'cone' one end by rolling it in the palms of your hands, then gently adding pressure on one end with the fingers of one hand. Use the pointed end of the Cel stick and the pointed end of a piping tube (nozzle) to add some buttons and other details.

7. Dab the bottom of the midsection with the sugar glue or water, then slide it down the piece of spaghetti until it rests on top of the trouser legs (Fig. 3).

8. Make a ball (see page 84) out of sugarpaste, marzipan or Mexican paste for

the head and, using the palms of your hands, roll it into an oval shape.

9. Using the tips of your fingers, gently pinch out the nose from the centre of the face (Fig. 4). Mark the nostrils, then hollow out the mouth with the pointed end of the Cel stick. Repeat for the eye sockets, dragging the Cel stick up slightly to create large cavities.

10. Make two small cones (see page 84) out of sugarpaste, marzipan or Mexican paste for the eyes. Dab the pointed ends of the

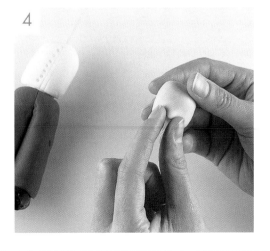

advanced decorating techniques

5

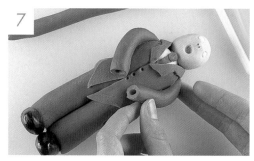

7

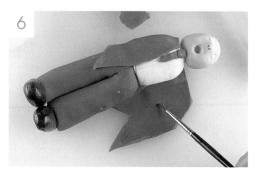

6

14. Form two small cones out of sugarpaste, marzipan or modelling paste for the hands. Flatten the wider end of each hand with your fingers, then use the knife to mark the fingers. You could also add some fingernails with the pointed end of a piping tube (nozzle). Dab the pointed ends of the hands with the sugar glue or water, then insert them into the ends of the arms.

cones with the sugar glue or water, then insert them into the eye sockets (Fig. 5). Dampen the underside of the head with the sugar glue or water and slide it down the piece of spaghetti, so it rests on top of the midsection.

11. For the tie, cut some rolled-out sugarpaste, marzipan or Mexican paste into any style you like. Dab the back with the sugar glue or water and attach it just below the head. A small, flattened ball at the top makes a good knot.

12. Make and attach the suit jacket and collar in the same way as the tie (see step 11) (Fig. 6).

13. Make two small cylinders out of sugarpaste, marzipan or Mexican paste for the arms, slicing off one end of each cylinder. Hollow out these ends – where the hands will be added later – with the pointed end of the Cel stick, and attach the arms to the body with the sugar glue or water (Fig. 7).

15. Paint some pupils on the eyes with paste food colouring, then add some eyelashes and eyebrows (Fig. 8).

16. Finish by piping on some hair with royal icing (Fig. 9).

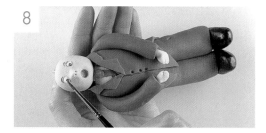

8

9

advanced decorating techniques

BALLERINA

1. Make two cylinders (see page 84) out of sugarpaste, marzipan or Mexican paste for the legs. Continue to roll the bottom half of each cylinder so that it narrows, then use a sharp knife to slice off the ends of both cylinders.

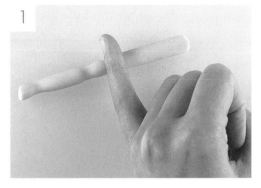

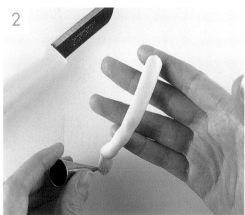

2. With your little finger, gently roll each cylinder 1 or 2cm (roughly ½in) above the narrow end to make the ankle. Repeat just above and below each cylinder's mid point to form the knee (Fig. 1). With the knife, slice a V behind one knee, so you can bend the leg. (This technique also works with arms.)

3. Flatten the narrow ends of the cylinders with your fingers to make the feet. Mark the toes with the knife, then use the pointed end of a piping tube (nozzle) to make the toenails (Fig. 2).

4. Set the legs in position on a piece of florist's oasis, which should be covered with cling film (plastic wrap) to prevent pieces flaking off (Fig. 3). Let the legs dry, then set them in place on a covered cake or board.

5. For the dress, make a cone (see page 84) out of sugarpaste, marzipan or Mexican paste and use the blunt end of a Cel stick to create the pleats. Start at the top of the cone

Techniques

Mouths can be formed in many different ways. For a round mouth, gently press a drinking straw with half of one end cut away into the face. To make an open mouth, press the pointed end of a piping tube (nozzle) into the face, then gently carve out the inside with a small, sharp knife. For a wide-open mouth, push the pointed end of a Cel stick or the end of a paintbrush handle into the face and drag it down. For a smiling mouth, take the wide end of a piping tube and rock the lower half against the face. For a frown, do the same, but use the upper half of the piping tube.

advanced decorating techniques

and drag the Cel stick downwards (Fig. 4). Then, hollow out the top of the dress with the Cel stick; the neck and shoulders will go here (Fig. 5).

6. Make another, smaller cone out of sugarpaste, marzipan or Mexican paste for the neck and shoulders, elongating the pointed end of the cone with your fingers. Using a paintbrush, dab the wider end of the cone with a little sugar glue or warm, previously boiled water and set it into the hollow in the dress (Fig. 6).

7. Cut some rolled-out sugarpaste, marzipan or Mexican paste into straps, sleeves or bows. Dab the backs with the sugar glue or water and set them in place on the shoulders. Add some detailing with the pointed end of the Cel stick, if you like (Fig. 7).

8. Make the arms in the same way that you made the legs in steps 1 to 3. Once they have dried, dab the tops with the sugar glue or water and attach them to the body.

9. Make a ball (see page 84) out of sugarpaste, marzipan or Mexican paste for the head and, with the palms of your hands, roll it into an oval shape. Set it onto a dowel and press this into the oasis. This will leave your hands free to focus on the facial features.

10. Using the tips of your fingers, gently pinch out the nose from the centre of the face. Mark the nostrils with the pointed end of the Cel stick. Hollow out the mouth, then repeat for the eye sockets, dragging the Cel stick upwards to create two large cavities.

11. Make two small cones out of sugarpaste, marzipan or Mexican paste. Dab the pointed ends of the cones with the sugar

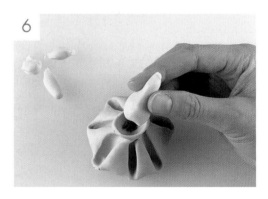

advanced decorating techniques

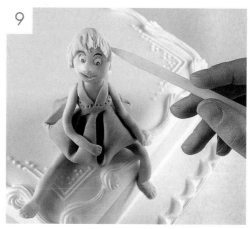

glue or water, then insert them into the eye sockets. Leave them to dry.

12. Paint some pupils on the eyes with a little paste food colouring, then add some eyelashes and eyebrows. You could also water down some paste food colouring and paint on the mouth. Remove the head from the dowel, dampen the underside with the sugar glue or water, then set it in place on the body (Fig. 8).

13. For the hair, take a small, marble-sized piece of sugarpaste, marzipan or Mexican

Techniques

Cup the ballerina's hands by moulding them round the blunt end of a Cel stick.

paste and flatten it. Dampen the underside with the sugar glue or water and attach it to the head. Using the pointed end of the Cel stick, mark the hair into any style you like (Fig. 9).

CHAPTER SIX

EASY TIERED WEDDING CAKES

The thought of making a tiered wedding cake can be daunting. All it requires, however, is a few extra pieces of equipment – dowels, a cake stand, pillars or a separator depending on the style of cake you are making – and the knowledge that you have acquired from the rest of this book.

Tiered Wedding Cakes

The most important thing to remember when you are making a tiered wedding cake is that the tiers must be in proportion (see chart below). If you are making a two-tiered cake, simply eliminate the top section. If you are attempting a four-tiered cake, make it to the following ratio: top tier, 15cm (6in); top middle tier, 20cm (8in); bottom middle tier, 25cm (10in); bottom tier, 30cm (12in).

RATIOS FOR TIERED CAKES

Top	Middle	Bottom
15cm (6in)	20cm (8in)	25cm (10in)
15cm (6in)	23cm (9in)	30cm (12in)
18cm (7in)	23cm (9in)	28cm (11in)

Using a Cake Stand

Cake stands offer the easiest method of displaying a tiered wedding cake. They are available at any sugarcraft or cook shop and come in two-, three- and four-tiered varieties, and in a range of designs.

To position covered cakes and boards on a cake stand, start with the largest, bottom tier and work your way up (Fig. 1). When everything is in place, decorate the cake with flowers so that it fits the colour scheme of the wedding, if you like (Fig. 2).

easy tiered wedding cakes

Using Pillars

Pillars must be supported by cake dowels, which carry the weight of the cake's tiers and prevent the pillars from sinking into the bottom tier. You can find dowels at any sugarcraft or cook shop.

1. Set the pillars in position on the bottom tier of the cake (see Troubleshooting, page 104, for the correct placement on round and square cakes). Insert a dowel in each pillar and push it down into the covered cake (Fig. 1).

2. Using a sharp knife, mark the points at which the dowels protrude from the pillars (Fig. 2).

3. Remove the dowels from the pillars one at a time and, using a hack saw, cut across them twice along the mark you made in step 2. The dowels should snap cleanly into two pieces.

Timesaving Tip

There is no need to make huge, multi-tiered wedding cakes if you are cooking for a large crowd. Simply make a cutting cake in addition to the wedding cake – it should be made from the same ingredients and covered and decorated in the same way – and keep it in the kitchen. No one will know that every single slice has not been cut from the main wedding cake.

Tools of the Trade

Pillars come in a variety of sizes and shapes, but 9cm (3½in) is the standard size for pillars used in a classic, three-tiered cake.

4. Insert the dowels back into the pillars (Fig. 3). They should now fit perfectly. If you find they are still too long, remove the dowels one at a time. Rub one end of each dowel with a piece of rough sandpaper until it is the right size, then insert it back into a pillar.

5. Set the next tier in position on top of the pillars and decorate both tiers with flowers, if you like (Fig. 4). If the cake is to have a top tier, simply repeat steps 1 to 5.

Troubleshooting

Never cluster dowels in the centre of a tiered cake. For square cakes, position the dowels in a rectangular or square shape 4cm (1½in) from the edges of the cake. For round cakes, position them in a triangular shape 4cm (1½in) from the edges of the cake.

3

4

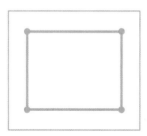

Troubleshooting

The top section of a tiered cake should never exceed 18cm (7in) or the cake will look as if it is missing its top tier.

easy tiered wedding cakes

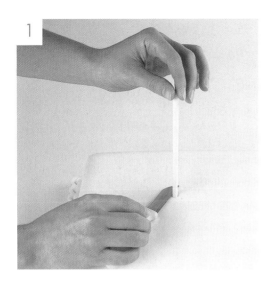

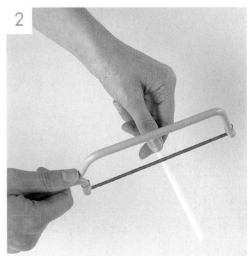

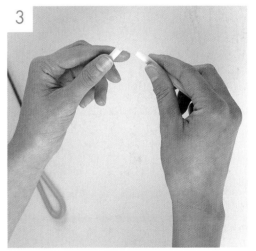

Using a Separator

Separators come in a wide range of makes and models but, like pillars, must always be supported by dowels.

1. Insert the dowels into the covered cake (see Troubleshooting, opposite, for the correct placement on round and square cakes). Using a sharp knife, mark the points at which the dowels protrude from the cake (Fig.1).

2. Remove the dowels from the cake one at a time and, using a hack saw, cut across them twice along the mark you made in step 1 (Fig. 2). The dowels should snap cleanly into two pieces (Fig. 3).

3. Insert the dowels back into the cake. They should now fit perfectly – but if you find they are still too long, remove them one at a time, rub one end of each dowel with a piece of rough sandpaper and insert it back into the cake (Fig. 4).

105

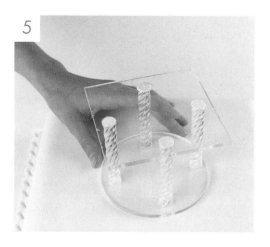

5

1

4. Set the separator on top of the dowels (Fig. 5). Place the next tier on top of this (Fig. 6), then decorate both tiers with flowers, if you like. If the cake is to have a top tier as well, repeat steps 1 to 4.

6

Making Stacked Cakes

Even stacked cakes, which do not appear to need any extra support, must be stabilized with cake dowels.

1. Follow steps 1 to 3 in Using a Separator (see page 105).

2. Set a 4-mm (⅛-in) board on top of the dowels, then place the next tier directly on top of this. If the cake is to have another tier, repeat steps 1 to 3 in Using a Separator, then set a 4-mm (⅛-in) board and the final tier on top of this.

3. Pipe some royal icing round the base of each tier to secure it, then finish the cake with some ribbons and flowers, if you like (Fig. 1).

easy tiered wedding cakes

CHAPTER SEVEN

THE ESSENTIALS

Storage and Transportation

Cutting Cakes

Portion Guide

Marzipan Guide

Sugarpaste (Rolled Fondant or
  Ready-to-Roll Icing) Guide

Recipes

Storage and Transportation

Always store cakes in cake boxes that fit the size of your boards. You can find cake boxes at any sugarcraft or cook shop, and they will keep your cakes dust-free while still allowing them to breathe. Try to leave cakes in out-of-the-way places that are neither too warm nor too cold; room temperature is ideal. Never, ever store them in the kitchen. The fluctuating temperatures and steam will quickly ruin all of your hard work.

Before you transport cakes, set them in cake boxes and seal the lids with masking or sticky tape to prevent them from flying off. Never place cakes on the front or back seat of your car. Car seats are sloped, so there is very little to stop them from sailing onto the floor if you have to brake suddenly. It is much better to set cakes on towels, blankets or non-slip matting, which you can find at any sugarcraft or cook shop, in the boot (trunk) of your car. Surround them with rolled-up towels to prevent them from shifting and to protect them from any other items that you might be storing in the boot.

Cutting Cakes

The standard fruit-cake portion for one person is 2.5cm (1in) squared. For a sponge cake, the standard portion is 5cm x 2.5cm squared (2in x 1in squared). The diagrams on the right show the best ways of cutting round and square cakes. When you cut the portions, be sure to use a good-quality, sharp knife without too much 'flex'.

If you are preparing to cut a cake that has been covered using the All-in-One method (see page 33), first slide a sharp knife round the base of the cake to free it from the board. This will make it much easier to lift and serve the portions later.

Cutting Round and Square Cakes

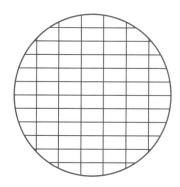

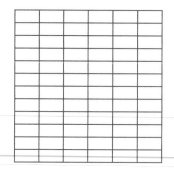

Thinking Ahead

If you know you are only going to use part of a cake, cut it straight down the middle. Slice equal-sized portions from the inner sides of both halves. Then, when you are finished, push what remains of the two halves together to prevent them from drying out.

Portion Guide

The following tables will help you to determine how many servings a cake will produce.

Round and Square Cakes

Fruit	Round/all other shapes except number and novelty cakes	Square	Sponge	Round/all other shapes except number and novelty cakes	Square
13cm (5in)	16	25	13cm (5in)	8	12
15cm (6in)	25	36	15cm (6in)	12	18
18cm (7in)	36	49	18cm (7in)	18	24
20cm (8in)	49	64	20cm (8in)	24	32
23cm (9in)	64	84	23cm (9in)	32	42
25cm (10in)	84	100	25cm (10in)	42	50
28cm (11in)	100	121	28cm (11in)	50	61
30cm (12in)	120	144	30cm (12in)	61	72
36cm (14$\frac{1}{4}$in)	144	196	36cm (14$\frac{1}{4}$in)	72	98
41cm (16$\frac{1}{4}$in)	196	256	41cm (16$\frac{1}{4}$in)	98	128

Number Cakes

Fruit		Sponge	
Number 0	20	Number 0	40
Number 1	15	Number 1	30
Numbers 2–9	20	Numbers 2–9	40

Novelty Cakes

Fruit/Sponge

Most novelty fruit cakes produce 50 portions, while novelty sponge cakes produce 25 to 30 portions. These numbers may sound impressive, but remember that novelty cakes are much shallower than those baked in ordinary tins (pans).

Marzipan Guide

This table will help you to work out how much marzipan you need to cover your cake.

Round and Square Cakes

Fruit	Round/all other shapes except number and novelty cakes	Square
13cm (5in)	275g (9½oz)	375g (13oz)
15cm (6in)	375g (13oz)	750g (1lb 10 oz)
18cm (7in)	750g (1lb 10 oz)	875g (2lb)
20cm (8in)	875g (2lb)	1kg (2lb 4oz)
23cm (9in)	1kg (2lb 4oz)	1.25kg (2lb 12oz)
25cm (10in)	1.25kg (2lb 12oz)	1.5kg (3lb 5oz)
28cm (11in)	1.5kg (3lb 5oz)	1.75kg (3lb 13oz)
30cm (12in)	1.75kg (3lb 13oz)	2kg (4lb 8oz)
36cm (14¼in)	2kg (4lb 8oz)	2.5kg (5lb 8oz)
41cm (16¼in)	2.5kg (5lb 8oz)	3kg (6lb 8oz)

Number Cakes

Fruit/Sponge

Number 0	1kg (2lb 4oz)
Number 1	875g (2lb)
Numbers 2–9	1kg (2lb 4oz)

Novelty Cakes

Fruit/Sponge

You will need 1kg (2lb 4oz) of marzipan to cover most novelty cakes.

Sugarpaste (Rolled Fondant or Ready-to-Roll Icing) Guide

This table will help you to work out how much sugarpaste (rolled fondant or ready-to-roll icing) you need to cover your cake.

Round and Square Cakes

	Round/all other shapes except number and novelty cakes	Square
13cm (5in)	375g (13oz)	500g (1lb 2oz)
15cm (6in)	500g (1lb 2oz)	875g (2lb)
18cm (7in)	875g (2lb)	1kg (2lb 4oz)
20cm (8in)	1kg (2lb 4oz)	1.25kg (2lb 12oz)
23cm (9in)	1.25kg (2lb 12oz)	1.5kg (3lb 5oz)
25cm (10in)	1.5kg (3lb 5oz)	1.75kg (3lb 13oz)
28cm (11in)	1.75kg (3lb 13oz)	2kg (4lb 8oz)
30cm (12in)	2kg (4lb 8oz)	2.5kg (5lb 8oz)
36cm (14¼in)	2.5kg (5lb 8oz)	3kg (6lb 8oz)
41cm (16¼in)	3kg (6lb 8oz)	3.5kg (8lb)

Number Cakes

Fruit/Sponge

Number 0	1.25kg (2lb 12oz)
Number 1	1kg (2lb 4oz)
Numbers 2–9	1.25kg (2lb 12oz)

Novelty Cakes

Fruit/Sponge

You will need 1.25kg (2lb 12oz) of sugarpaste to cover most novelty cakes.

RECIPES

In this section, ingredient quantities are given for 15cm (6in) round/12.5cm (5in) square cakes through to 32cm (13in) round/30cm (12in) square cakes for both the classic fruit and sponge cake recipes. For most variations of these recipes, however, ingredient quantities are only given for 13cm (5in) round/10cm (4in) square cakes to 20cm (8in) round/18cm (7in) square cakes. That is because these cakes are prone to flopping if they are made any larger. If you are baking for a large group, simply make more cakes, rather than increasing the sizes of the individual cakes.

Fruit Cakes

Fruit Cake see page 22 for recipe

Round/Square Cakes

ROUND	15cm	18cm	20cm	23cm	25cm	28cm	30cm	32cm
	(6in)	(7in)	(8in)	(9in)	(10in)	(11in)	(12in)	(13in)
SQUARE	13cm	15cm	18cm	20cm	23cm	25cm	28cm	30cm
	(5in)	(6in)	(7in)	(8in)	(9in)	(10in)	(11in)	(12in)
GLACÉ (CANDIED)	40g	65g	75g	100g	150g	225g	300g	350g
CHERRIES, CHOPPED	(1^1/2oz/3 tbsp)	(2^1/2oz/4 tbsp)	(2^3/4oz/^{1}/3 cup)	(3^1/2oz/^{1}/2 cup)	(5^1/2oz/^{3}/4 cup)	(8oz/1 cup)	(10^1/2oz/1^1/4 cups)	(12oz/1^1/2 cups)
CURRANTS	150g	220g	350g	450g	625g	775g	1.2kg	1.4kg
	(5^1/2oz/1 cup)	(8oz/1^1/4 cups)	(12oz/2 cups)	(1lb/3^1/2 cups)	(1lb 7oz/5 cups)	(1lb 12oz/5^3/4 cups)	(2lb 10oz/10^3/4 cups)	(3lb 5oz/11^1/4 cups)
SULTANAS	50g	90g	125g	200g	225g	375g	400g	500g
(GOLDEN RAISINS)	(1^3/4oz/^{1}/4 cup)	(3^1/4oz/^{1}/2 cup)	(4^1/2oz/^{3}/4 cup)	(7oz/1^1/4 cups)	(8oz/1^1/2 cups)	(13oz/1^3/4 cups)	(14oz/2^1/4 cups)	(1lb 2oz/3^3/4 cups)
RAISINS	50g	90g	125g	200g	225g	375g	400g	500g
	(1^3/4oz/^{1}/4 cup)	(3^1/4oz/^{1}/2 cup)	(4^1/2oz/^{3}/4 cup)	(7oz/1^1/4 cups)	(8oz/1^1/2 cups)	(13oz/1^3/4 cups)	(14oz/2^1/4 cups)	(1lb 2oz/3^3/4 cups)
MIXED FRUIT	25g	50g	50g	75g	100g	150g	200g	250g
PEEL	(1oz/^{1}/4 cup)	(1^3/4oz/^{1}/3 cup)	(1^3/4oz/^{1}/3 cup)	(2^3/4oz/^{1}/2 cup)	(3^1/2oz/^{3}/4 cup)	(5^1/2oz/1 cup)	(7oz/1^1/4 cups)	(9oz/1^3/4 cups)
LEMON RIND, GRATED	^{1}/2 lemon	^{1}/2 lemon	1 lemon	1 lemon	1 lemon	2 lemons	2 lemons	2 lemons
PLAIN (ALL-PURPOSE)	100g	175g	200g	350g	400g	600g	700g	825g
	(3^1/2oz/	(6oz/	(7oz/	(12oz/	(14oz/	(1lb 5oz/	(1lb 9oz/	(1lb 14oz/
FLOUR	^{3}/4 cup)	1^1/2 cups)	1^2/3 cups)	3 cups)	3^1/2 cups)	5^1/4 cups)	6^1/4 cups)	7^1/2 cups)
ALMONDS,	25g	50g	50g	50g	100g	150g	200g	250g
CHOPPED	(1oz/^{1}/4 cup)	(1^3/4oz/^{1}/2 cup)	(1^3/4oz/^{1}/2 cup)	(1^3/4oz/^{1}/2 cup)	(3^1/2oz/1 cup)	(5^1/2oz/1^1/2 cups)	(7oz/2 cups)	(9oz/2^1/4 cups)
GROUND CINNAMON	^{1}/4 tsp	^{1}/4 tsp	^{3}/4 tsp	1 tsp	1^1/4 tsp	1^1/4 tsp	1^1/2 tsp	1^3/4 tsp
NUTMEG	^{1}/4 tsp	^{1}/4 tsp	^{1}/2 tsp	^{1}/2 tsp	1 tsp	1 tsp	1^1/4 tsp	1^1/4 tsp
MIXED (PUMPKIN PIE) SPICE	^{1}/4 tsp	^{1}/4 tsp	^{1}/4 tsp	^{1}/2 tsp	1 tsp	1 tsp	1^1/4 sp	1^1/4 tsp
BUTTER/	75g	150g	175g	275g	350g	500g	600g	800g
MARGARINE	(2^3/4oz/	(5^1/2oz/	(6oz/	(9^1/2oz/	(12oz/	(1lb 2oz/	(1lb 5oz/	(1lb 12oz/
	^{1}/3 cup)	^{3}/4 cup)	^{3}/4 cup)	1^1/4 cups)	1^1/2 cups)	2^1/4 cups)	2^1/2 cups)	3^1/2 cups)
BROWN	75g	150g	175g	275g	350g	500g	600g	800g
SUGAR	(2^3/4 oz/	(5^1/2oz/	(6oz/	(9^1/2oz/	(12oz/	(1lb 2oz/	(1lb 5oz/	(1lb 12oz/
	^{1}/2 cup)	1 cup)	1^1/4 cups)	1^3/4 cups)	2^1/4 cups)	3 cups)	3^1/2 cups)	4^3/4 cups)
EGGS	2	3	4	5	6	9	11	14
BLACK TREACLE (MOLASSES)	1 tsp	1 tsp	1 tbsp	1 tbsp	1 tbsp	2 tbsp	2 tbsp	2 tbsp
Approximate baking time at 120°C/250°F/Gas Mark 1/2								
	2 hours	2^1/2 hours	3 hours	3^1/4 hours	3^3/4 hours	4^1/2 hours	5^1/2 hours	6^1/2 hours

111

Gluten-Free Fruit Cake

If you would like to make this fruit cake even richer, increase the quantity of dried fruit and cherries used to taste.

Gluten-Free Fruit Cake
Round/Square Cakes

Round	13cm	15cm	18cm	20cm
	(5in)	(6in)	(7in)	(8in)
Square	10cm	13cm	15cm	18cm
	(4in)	(5in)	(6in)	(7in)
Water/Apple or	70ml	125ml	190ml	250ml
Pineapple juice	(5 tbsp)	(8 tbsp)	(7 fl oz/1 cup)	(9 fl oz/1 cup)
Brown/White sugar	25g	55g	85g	115g
	(1oz/$^1\!/_4$ cup)	(2oz/$^1\!/_2$ cup)	(3oz/$^3\!/_4$ cup)	(4oz/1 cup)
Vegetable margarine	175g	225g	350g	450g
(shortening)	(6oz/$^3\!/_4$ cup)	(8oz/1 cup)	(12oz/1$^1\!/_2$ cups)	(1lb/2 cups)
Dried fruit	175g	225g	350g	450g
	(6oz/1 cup)	(8oz/1$^1\!/_2$ cups)	(12oz/1$^3\!/_4$ cups)	(1lb/3 cups)
Glacé (candied)	25g	40g	55g	55g
cherries	(1oz/3 tbsp)	(1$^1\!/_2$oz/3 tbsp)	(2oz/$^1\!/_2$ cup)	(2oz/$^1\!/_2$ cup)
Gluten-free flour	70g	85g	150g	200g
	(2$^1\!/_2$oz/9 tbsp)	(3oz/$^2\!/_3$ cup)	(5$^1\!/_2$oz/1$^1\!/_4$ cups)	(7oz/1$^2\!/_3$ cups)
Mixed (pumpkin pie) spice	$^1\!/_4$ tsp	$^1\!/_2$ tsp	$^3\!/_4$ tsp	1 tsp
Ground almonds	40g	55g	85g	85g
	(1$^1\!/_2$oz/$^1\!/_4$ cup)	(2oz/$^1\!/_2$ cup)	(3oz/$^3\!/_4$ cup)	(3oz/$^3\!/_4$ cup)
Eggs	1	1	2	2
Approximate baking time at 120°C/250°F/Gas Mark 1/2				
	45mins	60mins	75mins	90mins

METHOD

1. Put the water/apple or pineapple juice, brown/white sugar, vegetable margarine (shortening), dried fruit and glacé (candied) cherries in a pan (saucepan) and boil.

2. Continue boiling for approximately 10 minutes, then remove the mixture from the heat and leave it to cool.

3. Blend in the gluten-free flour, mixed (pumpkin pie) spice, ground almonds and eggs, plus a little more water/fruit juice if necessary to soften the mixture.

4. Spoon the mixture into a lined tin (pan), then use the spoon to create a slight depression in the centre of the mixture. This helps to keep the cake level as it bakes.

the essentials

Egg-Free Fruit Cake

If you would like to make this fruit cake even richer, increase the quantity of dried fruit and cherries used to taste.

Egg-Free Fruit Cake
Round/Square Cakes

ROUND	13cm	15cm	18cm	20cm
	(5in)	(6in)	(7in)	(8in)
SQUARE	10cm	13cm	15cm	18cm
	(4in)	(5in)	(6in)	(7in)
WATER/APPLE OR	70ml	125ml	190ml	250ml
PINEAPPLE JUICE	(5 tbsp)	(8 tbsp)	(7 fl oz/1 cup)	(9 fl oz/1 cup)
BROWN/WHITE SUGAR	25g	55g	85g	115g
	(1oz/^{1}/4 cup)	(2oz/^{1}/2 cup)	(3oz/^{3}/4 cup)	(4oz/1 cup)
VEGETABLE MARGARINE (SHORTENING)	175g	225g	350g	450g
	(6oz/^{3}/4 cup)	(8oz/1 cup)	(12oz/1^1/2 cups)	(1lb/2 cups)
DRIED FRUIT	175g	225g	350g	450g
	(6oz/1 cup)	(8oz/1^1/2 cups)	(12oz/1^3/4 cups)	(1lb/3 cups)
GLACÉ (CANDIED) CHERRIES	25g	40g	55g	55g
	(1oz/3 tbsp)	(1^1/2oz/3 tbsp)	(2oz/^{1}/2 cup)	(2oz/^{1}/2 cup)
SELF-RAISING (SELF-RISING) FLOUR	55g	85g	175g	225g
	(2oz/^{1}/2 cup)	(3oz/^{2}/3 cup)	(6oz/1^1/2 cups)	(8oz/2 cups)
MIXED (PUMPKIN PIE) SPICE	1.25ml	2.5ml	5ml	5ml
	(^{1}/4 tsp)	(^{1}/2 tsp)	(1 tsp)	(1 tsp)
GROUND ALMONDS (optional)	25g	40g	55g	55g
	(1oz/^{1}/4 cup)	(1^1/2oz/^{1}/4 cup)	(2oz/^{1}/2 cup)	(2oz/^{1}/2 cup)
Approximate baking time at 120°C/250°F/Gas Mark 1/2				
	45mins	60mins	75mins	90mins

METHOD

1. Put the water/apple or pineapple juice, brown/white sugar, vegetable margarine (shortening), dried fruit and glacé (candied) cherries in a pan (saucepan)and boil.
2. Continue boiling for approximately 10 minutes, then remove the mixture from the heat and leave it to cool.
3. Blend in the self-raising (self-rising) flour, mixed (pumpkin pie) spice and ground almonds, if used, plus a little more water/fruit juice if necessary to soften the mixture.
4. Spoon the mixture into a lined tin (pan), then use the spoon to create a slight depression in the centre of the mixture. This helps to keep the cake level as it bakes.

113

Dairy-Free Fruit Cake

Make the fruit cake recipe on page 22 (see ingredient quantities, page 111) dairy free by substituting vegetable margarine (shortening) for the ordinary margarine.

Diabetic Fruit Cake

If you would like to make this fruit cake even richer, increase the quantity of dried fruit and cherries used to taste.

Diabetic Fruit Cake
Round/Square Cakes

ROUND	13cm	15cm	18cm	20cm
	(5in)	(6in)	(7in)	(8in)
SQUARE	10cm	13cm	15cm	18cm
	(4in)	(5in)	(6in)	(7in)
PLAIN (ALL-PURPOSE) FLOUR	85g	115g	140g	200g
	(3oz/^{2}/3 cup)	(4oz/1 cup)	(5oz/1^1/4 cups)	(7oz/1^2/3 cups)
SALT	^{1}/4 tsp	^{1}/4 tsp	^{1}/2 tsp	^{1}/2 tsp
CINNAMON	^{1}/2 tsp	^{1}/2 tsp	1 tsp	1 tsp
MIXED (PUMPKIN PIE) SPICE	^{1}/2 tsp	^{1}/2 tsp	1 tsp	1 tsp
NUTMEG	^{1}/2 tsp	^{1}/2 tsp	^{1}/2 tsp	^{1}/2 tsp
RAISINS	225g	200g	225g	280g
	(8oz/1^1/2 cups)	(7oz/1^1/4 cups)	(8oz/1^1/2 cups)	(10oz/1^3/4 cups)
CURRANTS	225g	200g	225g	280g
	(8oz/1^1/4 cups)	(7oz/1^1/4 cups)	(8oz/1^1/4 cups)	(10oz/1^1/2 cups)
SULTANAS (GOLDEN RAISINS)	225g	200g	225g	280g
	(8oz/1^1/2 cups)	(7oz/1^1/4 cups)	(8oz/1^1/2 cups)	(10oz/1^3/4 cups)
GLACÉ (CANDIED) CHERRIES	115g	85g	115g	175g
	(4oz/^{1}/2 cup)	(3oz/^{1}/3 cup)	(4oz/^{1}/2 cup)	(6oz/^{3}/4 cup)
FLAKED (SLIVERED) ALMONDS	115g	85g	115g	175g
	(4oz/1^1/3 cups)	(3oz/1 cup)	(4oz/1^1/3 cups)	(6oz/1^1/2 cups)
POLYUNSATURATED MARGARINE	140g	115g	140g	175g
	(5oz/^{1}/2 cup)	(4oz/^{1}/2 cup)	(5oz/^{1}/2 cup)	(6oz/^{3}/4 cup)
SOFT BROWN SUGAR	55g	115g	55g	55g
	(2oz/^{1}/2 cup)	(4oz/1 cup)	(2oz/^{1}/2 cup)	(2oz/^{1}/2 cup)
EGGS	4	3	4	5
BICARBONATE OF (BAKING) SODA	^{1}/2 tsp	^{3}/4 tsp	1 tsp	1^1/2 tsp
WARM WATER	5ml	7.5ml	10ml	15ml
	(1 tsp)	(1^1/2 tsp)	(2 tsp)	(1 tbsp)
BRANDY (optional)	75ml	60ml	75ml	105ml
	(5 tbsp)	(4 tbsp)	(5 tbsp)	(7 tbsp)
Approximate baking time at 150°C/300°F/Gas Mark 2				
	90mins	120mins	150mins	180mins

METHOD

1. In a mixing bowl, blend the plain (all-purpose) flour, salt, cinnamon, mixed (pumpkin pie) spice, nutmeg, raisins, currants, sultanas (golden raisins), glacé (candied) cherries and flaked (slivered) almonds.

2. In a separate bowl, stir together the polyunsaturated margarine and soft brown sugar.

3. Gradually add the eggs and the dry ingredients from step 1 to the margarine mixture.

4. Dissolve the bicarbonate of soda (baking soda) in the warm water, then add this to the margarine mixture. To soften its consistency, add a little more water, 15ml (1 tbsp) at a time.

5. Spoon the mixture into a lined cake tin (pan) and level it. After baking, drizzle the fruit cake with the brandy, if used.

Sponge Cakes

Sponge Cake see page 23 for recipe

Round/Square Cakes

ROUND	15cm	18cm	20cm	23cm	25cm	28cm	30cm	32cm
	(6in)	(7in)	(8in)	(9in)	(10in)	(11in)	(12in)	(13in)
SQUARE	13cm	15cm	18cm	20cm	23cm	25cm	28cm	30cm
	(5in)	(6in)	(7in)	(8in)	(9in)	(10in)	(11in)	(12in)
BUTTER/	225g	275g	336g	450g	616g	700g	730g	787g
MARGARINE	(8oz/1 cup)	(9½oz/1¼ cups)	(11½oz/1½ cups)	(1lb/2 cups)	(1lb 5oz/2½ cups)	(1lb 9oz/3 cups)	(1lb 10oz/3¼ cups)	(1lb 2oz/3½ cups)
CASTER (SUPERFINE)	225g	275g	336g	450g	616g	700g	730g	787g
SUGAR	(8oz/1 cup)	(9½oz/1¼cups)	(11½oz/1½cups)	(1lb/2¼ cups)	(1lb 5oz/2¾ cups)	(1lb 9oz/3 cups)	(1lb 10oz/3¼ cups)	(1lb 12oz/3½ cups)
EGGS	4	5	6	8	10	12	13	14
SELF-RAISING	225g	275g	336g	450g	616g	700g	730g	787g
(SELF-RISING) FLOUR	(8oz/2 cups)	(9½oz/2¼ cups)	(11½oz/3 cups)	(1lb/4 cups)	(1lb 5oz/5¼ cups)	(1lb 9oz/6¼ cups)	(1lb 10oz/6½ cups)	(1lb 12oz/7 cups)
MILK/WATER	5ml	5ml	10ml	10ml	10ml	20ml	20ml	30ml
	(1tsp)	(1tsp)	(2 tsp)	(2 tsp)	(2 tsp)	(4 tsp)	(4 tsp)	(2 tbsp)
Approximate baking time at 120°C/250°F/Gas Mark 1/2								
	40mins	40min sq/ 50mins rd	50mins	60mins	60mins sq/ 85mins rd	85mins	95mins	95mins

Number Cakes

For sponge cakes baked in number 0 and 2–9 frames, use the ingredient quantities for the 15cm (6in) round/13cm (5in) square cake for a shallow cake, and the ingredient quantities for the 18cm (7in) round/15cm (6in) square cake for a deeper cake. For sponge cakes baked in a number 1 frame, use 175g (6oz) of all dry ingredients, 3 eggs and 5ml (1 tsp) of milk or water. Bake number 1–5, 7 and 8 cakes for 40 minutes, and number 0, 6 and 9 cakes for 45 minutes.

Novelty Cakes

For all sponge cakes baked in novelty tins (pans), use the ingredient quantities for either the 18cm (7in) round/15cm (6in) square cake or the 20cm (8in) round/18cm (7in) square cake. The latter guarantees a deeper cake.

SPONGE CAKE FLAVOUR VARIATIONS

Chocolate Blend 2 heaped tablespoons of cocoa powder with the milk/water used in the sponge cake recipe on page 23 (see ingredient quantities on page 115). For a marbled effect, make half of the sponge cake as in the recipe on page 23 (see ingredient quantities on page 115), and half of it with chocolate flavouring. Add the two mixtures to the tin (pan) in alternate spoonfuls, then run a knife through the ingredients to create the marbling.

Chocolate Chip Add a handful of chocolate chips to the sponge cake recipe on page 23 (see ingredient quantities on page 115).

Coffee Blend a level tablespoon of instant or liquid coffee with the milk/water used in the sponge cake recipe on page 23 (see ingredient quantities on page 115). You could also add a handful of walnuts, if you like.

Lemon Add the grated rind and juice from 1 lemon to the sponge cake recipe on page 23 (see ingredient quantities on page 115).

Orange Add the grated rind and juice from 1 orange to the sponge cake recipe on page 23 (see ingredient quantities on page 115). Add the grated rind and juice from both 1 orange and 1 lemon for a lovely St Clement's cake.

Gluten-Free Sponge Cake

This cake should be cooked in two halves to prevent it from flopping. You will need two lined tins (pans) of the same size; if you only have one tin, halve the mixture and cook one half at a time.

Gluten-Free Sponge Cake
Round/Square Cakes

ROUND	15cm (6in)	18cm (7in)	20cm (8in)	23cm (9in)	25cm (10in)	28cm (11in)
SQUARE	13cm (5in)	15cm (6in)	18cm (7in)	20cm (8in)	23cm (9in)	25cm (10in)
GLUTEN-FREE FLOUR	150g (5½oz/1½ cups)	200g (7oz/1⅔ cups)	250g (9oz/2¼ cups)	350g (12oz/3 cups)	425g (15oz/3⅔ cups)	500g (1lb 2oz/4½ cups)
GROUND ALMONDS	50g (1¾oz/½ cup)	50g (1¾oz/½ cup)	75g (2¾oz/½ cup)	100g (3½oz/¾ cup)	150g (5½oz/1 cup)	175g (6oz/1¼ cups)
VEGETABLE MARGARINE (SHORTENING)	200g (7oz/1 cup)	250g (9oz/1¼ cups)	350g (12oz/1½ cups)	450g (1lb/2¼ cups)	600g (1lb 5oz/2¾ cups)	700g (1lb 9oz/3 cups)
CASTER (SUPERFINE) SUGAR	200g (7oz/1 cup)	250g (9oz/1¼ cups)	350g (12oz/1¾ cups)	450g (1lb/2 cups)	600g (1lb 5oz/2½ cups)	700g (1lb 9oz/3 cups)
EGGS	4	5	6	8	10	12
WARM WATER (optional)						

Bake the cake for approximately 45 minutes at 120°C/250°F/Gas Mark 1/2.

METHOD

1. Blend the gluten-free flour and ground almonds in a mixing bowl and set it aside.

2. In a separate bowl, cream the vegetable margarine (shortening) and caster (superfine) sugar until the mixture is light and creamy, and the colour has visibly lightened.

3. Scrape down the bowl and give the mixture one more quick stir, then gradually add the flour mixture and the eggs.

4. If necessary, add just enough warm water to soften the mixture.

the essentials

Egg-Free Sponge Cake

This cake should be cooked in two halves to prevent it from flopping. You will need two lined tins (pans) of the same size; if you only have one tin, halve the mixture and cook one half at a time.

Egg-Free Sponge Cake
Round/Square Cakes

ROUND	13cm	15cm	18cm	20cm
	(5in)	(6in)	(7in)	(8in)
SQUARE	10cm	13cm	15cm	18cm
	(4in)	(5in)	(6in)	(7in)
VEGETABLE MARGARINE	25g	30g	40g	50g
(SHORTENING)	(1oz/2 tbsp)	(1oz/2 tbsp)	(1^1/2oz/^{1}/4 cup)	(1^3/4oz/^{1}/4 cup)
SUGAR	50g	65g	80g	100g
	(1^3/4oz/^{1}/4 cup)	(2^1/2oz/^{1}/4 cup)	(3oz/^{1}/2 cup)	(3^1/2oz/^{1}/2 cup)
GOLDEN (CORN) SYRUP	50g	65g	80g	100g
	(1^3/4oz/^{1}/4 cup)	(2^1/2oz/^{1}/4 cup)	(3oz/^{1}/2 cup)	(3^1/2oz/^{1}/2 cup)
BICARBONATE OF (BAKING) SODA	^{1}/4 tsp	^{1}/2 tsp	^{3}/4 tsp	1 tsp
MILK	125ml	150ml	200ml	300ml
	(4fl oz/^{1}/2 cup)	(5fl oz/^{1}/2 cup)	(7fl oz/1 cup)	(10fl oz/1^1/4 cups)
SELF-RAISING (RISING) FLOUR	175g	230g	280g	350g
	(6oz/1^1/2 cups)	(9oz/2^1/4 cups)	(10oz/2^1/2 cups)	(12oz/3 cups)
SALT	to taste	to taste	to taste	to taste
COCOA POWDER	25g	30g	40g	50g
	(1oz/^{1}/4 cup)	(1oz/^{1}/4 cup)	(1^1/2oz/^{1}/2 cup)	(1^3/4 oz/^{1}/2 cup)

Approximate baking time at 190°C/375°F/Gas Mark 5

	20mins	25mins	30mins	40mins

METHOD

1. Cream together the vegetable margarine (shortening), sugar and golden (corn) syrup in a mixing bowl.

2. In a separate bowl, dissolve the bicarbonate of soda (baking soda) in the milk.

3. Blend the self-raising (self-rising) flour, salt and cocoa powder in another bowl, then alternately add the margarine and bicarbonate of soda (baking soda) mixtures. You should end up with a thick batter.

4. Divide the mixture equally between the two lined tins (pans), then bake immediately.

Gluten-, Dairy- and Egg-Free Sponge Cake

This cake should be cooked in two halves to prevent it from flopping. You will need two lined tins (pans) of the same size; if you only have one tin, halve the mixture and cook one half at a time.

Gluten-, Dairy- and Egg-Free Sponge Cake

Round/Square Cakes

ROUND	13cm	15cm	18cm	20cm
	(5in)	(6in)	(7in)	(8in)
SQUARE	10cm	13cm	15cm	18cm
	(4in)	(5in)	(6in)	(7in)
DAIRY-FREE MARGARINE	25g	30g	40g	50g
	(1oz/2 tbsp)	(1oz/2 tbsp)	(1^1/2oz/^{1}/4 cup)	(1^3/4oz/^{1}/4 cup)
SUGAR	50g	65g	80g	100g
	(1^3/4oz/^{1}/4 cup)	(2^1/2oz/^{1}/4 cup)	(3oz/^{1}/2 cup)	(3^1/2oz/^{1}/2 cup)
GOLDEN (CORN) SYRUP	50g	65g	80g	100g
	(1^3/4oz/^{1}/4 cup)	(2^1/2oz/^{1}/4 cup)	(3oz/^{1}/2 cup)	(3^1/2oz/^{1}/2 cup)
BICARBONATE OF (BAKING) SODA	1 tsp	1^1/4 tsp	1^1/2 tsp	2 tsp
SOYA MILK	125ml	150ml	200ml	300ml
	(4fl oz/^{1}/2 cup)	(5fl oz/^{1}/2 cup)	(7fl oz/1 cup)	(10fl oz/1^1/4 cups)
GLUTEN-FREE FLOUR	175g	230g	280g	350g
	(6oz/1^1/2 cups)	(9oz/2^1/4 cups)	(10oz/2^1/2 cups)	(12oz/3 cups)
SALT	to taste	to taste	to taste	to taste
COCOA POWDER	25g	30g	40g	50g
(Optional)	(^{1}/2oz/^{1}/4 cup)	(1oz/^{1}/4 cup)	(1^1/2oz/^{1}/2 cup)	(1^3/4oz/^{1}/2 cup)
Approximate baking time at 190°C/375°F/Gas Mark 5				
	20mins	25mins	30mins	40mins

METHOD

1. Cream together the dairy-free margarine, sugar and golden (corn) syrup in a mixing bowl.
2. In a separate bowl, dissolve the bicarbonate of soda (baking soda) in the soya milk.
3. Blend the gluten-free flour, salt and cocoa powder, if used, in another bowl, then alternately add the margarine and bicarbonate of soda (baking soda) mixtures. You should end up with a thick batter.
4. Divide the mixture equally between the two lined tins (pans), then bake immediately.

118

Dairy-Free Sponge Cake

Make the sponge cake recipe on page 23 (see ingredient quantities, page 115) dairy free by substituting water for the milk, and vegetable margarine (shortening) for the butter/ordinary margarine.

DAIRY-FREE CHOCOLATE TOPPING
If you wish to use this topping as a filling as well, double the quantity of all ingredients.

METHOD
1. Break up the dairy-free plain (dark) chocolate and add it to a stainless-steel mixing bowl with the vegetable margarine (shortening) and soya milk.
2. Set the bowl over a pan (saucepan) of boiling water and reduce the heat. Stir the mixture until it is completely melted.
4. Add the icing (confectioners') sugar and blend until smooth.
5. Apply to the cake immediately.

Dairy-Free Chocolate Topping
Round/Square Cakes

ROUND	13cm	15cm	18cm	20cm
	(5in)	(6in)	(7in)	(8in)
SQUARE	10cm	13cm	15cm	18cm
	(4in)	(5in)	(6in)	(7in)
DAIRY-FREE PLAIN (DARK)	25g	50g	75g	100g
CHOCOLATE	(1oz)	(1^3/$_4$oz)	(2^3/$_4$oz)	(3^1/$_2$oz)
VEGETABLE MARGARINE	13g	25g	38g	50g
(SHORTENING)	(^{1}/$_2$oz/1 tbsp)	(1oz/2 tbsp)	(1^1/$_2$oz/^{1}/$_4$ cup)	(1^3/$_4$oz/^{1}/$_4$ cup)
SOYA MILK	13ml	25ml	38ml	50ml
	(1 tbsp)	(2 tbsp)	(3 tbsp)	(3 tbsp)
ICING (CONFECTIONERS') SUGAR	45g	90g	135g	175g
	(1^3/$_4$oz/^{1}/$_2$ cup)	(3^1/$_4$oz/^{3}/$_4$ cup)	(5oz/1 cup)	(6oz/1^1/$_4$ cups)

Diabetic Sponge Cake

It is strongly recommended that you divide this cake mixture into two lined tins (pans) of equal size to achieve the baking times in the chart overleaf. If you only have one tin, halve the mixture and cook one half at a time.

Remember to only use diabetic jam (jelly) and cream filling (see recipe, overleaf) in this sponge cake; the sugar content in ordinary jam and buttercream recipes is far too high for diabetics.

Diabetic Sponge Cake
Round/Square Cakes

ROUND	13cm (5in)	15cm (6in)	18cm (7in)	20cm (8in)
SQUARE	10cm (4in)	13cm (5in)	15cm (6in)	18cm (7in)
LOW-FAT MARGARINE	85g (3oz/½ cup)	175g (6oz/¾ cup)	265g (9½oz/1¼ cups)	350g (12oz/1½ cups)
CASTER (SUPER-FINE) SUGAR/ SUGAR SUBSTITUTE	40g (1½oz/¼ cup)	75g (2¾oz/¼ cup)	115g (4oz/½ cup)	150g (5½oz/1¼ cups)
EGGS	2	3	4–5	6
SELF-RAISING (SELF-RISING) FLOUR	85g (3oz/⅔ cup)	175g (6oz/1½cups)	265g (9½oz/2¼ cups)	350g (12oz/3 cups)
HOT WATER	15–20ml (1 tbsp)	30–40ml (2–3 tbsp)	50–60ml (3–4 tbsp)	70–80ml (5 tbsp)
VANILLA ESSENCE (EXTRACT) (optional)	to taste	to taste	to taste	to taste
Approximate baking time at 170°C/350°F/Gas Mark 4	20mins	25mins	30mins	40mins

METHOD

1. In a mixing bowl, cream together the low-fat margarine and caster (superfine) sugar/sugar substitute until the mixture is white and fluffy.
2. Stir in one egg at a time with a little of the self-raising (self-rising) flour, until all of the eggs and flour have been incorporated. Add the hot water and a little vanilla essence (extract), if necessary, to soften the mixture.
3. Divide the mixture equally between two lined tins (pans), then bake immediately.

DIABETIC CREAM FILLING

As the artificial sweetener in this recipe has a very strong taste, blend the filling and apply a thin layer to the cake just before it is to be eaten. The flavourings below also help to disguise the taste of the artificial sweetener.

FLAVOURINGS FOR DIABETIC CREAM FILLING
Coffee Add just enough water to 1 teaspoon of instant coffee to dissolve it, then mix this into the diabetic cream filling.
Chocolate Blend 2 teaspoons of cocoa powder into the diabetic cream filling.

Diabetic Cream Filling
Round/Square Cakes

ROUND	13cm (5in)	15cm (6in)	18cm (7in)	20cm (8in)
SQUARE	10cm (4in)	13cm (5in)	15cm (6in)	18cm (7in)
ARTIFICIAL SWEETENER	30ml (2 tbsp)	60ml (4 tbsp)	90ml (6 tbsp)	120ml (8 tbsp)
LOW-FAT MARGARINE	25g (1oz/ 2 tbsp)	50g (1¾oz/ ¼ cup)	75g (2¾oz/ ⅓ cup)	120g (4½oz/ ½ cup)

Buttercream

See the recipe on page 26 for the method. The quantities below will give you enough buttercream to fill and cover the tops and sides of your cakes.

Buttercream Icing
Round/Square Cakes

ROUND	13cm	15cm	18cm	20cm
	(5in)	(6in)	(7in)	(8in)
SQUARE	10cm	13cm	15cm	18cm
	(4in)	(5in)	(6in)	(7in)
BUTTER/MARGARINE	60g	125g	180g	250g
	(2¼oz/4 tbsp)	(4½oz/½ cup)	(6oz/¾ cup)	(9oz/1 cup)
ICING (CONFECTIONERS')	250g	500g	750g	1kg
SUGAR	(9oz/1¾ cups)	(1lb 2oz/3¼ cups)	(1lb 10oz/5 cups)	(2lb 4oz/7 cups)
HOT WATER	10ml	20ml	30ml	40ml
	(2 tsp)	(4 tsp)	(2 tbsp)	(2½ tbsp)

Marzipan

See the recipe on page 30 for the method, and the Marzipan Quantity Guide on page 110 for the amount of marzipan needed to cover different-sized cakes.

The quantities below will give you enough marzipan to cover the tops and sides of your cakes.

Marzipan
Round/Square Cakes

ROUND	13cm	15cm	18cm	20cm
	(5in)	(6in)	(7in)	(8in)
SQUARE	10cm	13cm	15cm	18cm
	(4in)	(5in)	(6in)	(7in)
GROUND ALMONDS	115g	225g	350g	450g
	(4oz/	(8oz/	(12oz/	(1lb/
	¾ cup)	1½ cups)	2½ cups)	3¼ cups)
ICING (CONFECTIONERS')	55g	115g	175g	225g
SUGAR	(2oz/½cup)	(4oz/1 cup)	(6oz/1½ cups)	(8oz/2 cups)
CASTER (SUPERFINE) SUGAR	55g	115g	175g	225g
	(2oz/¼ cup)	(4oz/½ cup)	(6oz/¾ cup)	(8oz/1 cup)
EGG YOLKS	2	4	6	8
RUM/BRANDY (optional)	3ml	5ml	8ml	10ml
	(½ tsp)	(1 tsp)	(1½ tsp)	(2 tsp)

Egg-Free Marzipan

See the Marzipan Quantity Guide on page 110 for the amount of marzipan needed to cover different-sized cakes.

The quantities below will give you enough egg-free marzipan to cover the tops and sides of your cakes.

Egg-Free Marzipan
Round/Square Cakes

ROUND	13cm	15cm	18cm	20cm
	(5in)	(6in)	(7in)	(8in)
SQUARE	10cm	13cm	15cm	18cm
	(4in)	(5in)	(6in)	(7in)
ICING (CONFECTIONERS') SUGAR	250g	500g	750g	1kg
	(9oz/1^3/4 cups)	(1lb 2oz/3^1/4 cups)	(1lb 10oz/5 cups)	(2lb 4oz/7 cups)
WATER	125ml	250ml	375ml	500ml
	(4fl oz/^{1}/2 cup)	(9fl oz/1 cup)	(13fl oz/1^1/2 cups)	(18fl oz/2^1/4 cups)
CREAM OF TARTAR	pinch	0.5ml	2ml	2ml
		(^{1}/8 tsp)	(^{1}/2 tsp)	(^{1}/2 tsp)
GROUND ALMONDS	75g	125g	190g	250g
	(2^3/4oz/^{1}/2 cup)	(4^1/2oz/1 cup)	(7oz/1^1/2 cups)	(9oz/1^3/4 cups)
LIQUID GLUCOSE	15ml	22.5ml	30ml	30ml
	(1 tbsp)	(1^1/2 tbsp)	(2 tbsp)	(2 tbsp)
ESSENCE (EXTRACT) OF YOUR CHOICE (optional)	2.5ml	5ml	7.5ml	10ml
	(^{1}/2 tsp)	(1 tsp)	(1^1/2 tsp)	(2 tsp)

METHOD

1. Put the icing (confectioners') sugar and water in a pan (saucepan) and dissolve the sugar over a low heat.

2. Once it has dissolved completely, raise the heat to 120°C/250°F until the water boils.

3. Remove the mixture from the heat and leave it to cool for 20 minutes.

4. Add the cream of tartar, ground almonds, liquid glucose and essence (extract), if used, and beat until the mixture is thick and creamy.

5. Leave the mixture to cool completely, then turn it out onto a clean work surface and knead until it is smooth.

Nut-Free Marzipan

See the Marzipan Quantity Guide on page 110 for the amount of marzipan needed to cover different-sized cakes.

The quantities below will give you enough nut-free marzipan to cover the tops and sides of your cakes.

Nut-Free Marzipan
Round/Square Cakes

ROUND	13cm	15cm	18cm	20cm
	(5in)	(6in)	(7in)	(8in)
SQUARE	10cm	13cm	15cm	18cm
	(4in)	(5in)	(6in)	(7in)
ICING (CONFECTIONERS')	250g	500g	750g	1kg
SUGAR	(9oz/1³/4 cups)	(1lb 2oz/3¹/4 cups)	(1lb 10oz/5 cups)	(2lb 4oz/7 cups)
WATER	125ml	250ml	375ml	500ml
	(4fl oz/¹/2 cup)	(9fl oz/1 cup)	(13fl oz/1¹/2 cups)	(18fl oz/2¹/4 cups)
CREAM OF TARTAR	pinch	0.5ml	2ml	2ml
		(¹/8 tsp)	(¹/2 tsp)	(¹/2 tsp)
GROUND RICE	75g	125g	190g	250g
	(2³/4oz/¹/2 cup)	(4¹/2oz/1 cup)	(7oz/1¹/2 cups)	(9oz/1³/4 cups)
EGGS	1	1	2	2
ESSENCE (EXTRACT) OF YOUR	2.5ml	5ml	7.5ml	10ml
CHOICE (optional)	(¹/2 tsp)	(1 tsp)	(1¹/2 tsp)	(2 tsp)

METHOD

1. Put the icing (confectioners') sugar and water in a pan (saucepan) and dissolve the sugar over a low heat.

2. Once it has dissolved completely, raise the heat to 120°C/250°F until the water boils.

3. Remove the mixture from the heat and leave it to cool for 20 minutes.

4. Add the cream of tartar, ground rice, egg and essence (extract), if used, and beat the mixture until thick and creamy.

5. Leave the mixture to cool completely, then turn it out onto a clean work surface and knead until it is smooth.

123

the essentials

Sugarpaste (Rolled Fondant or Ready-to-Roll Icing)

See the recipe on page 32 for the method, and the Sugarpaste (Rolled Fondant or Ready-to-Roll Icing) Quantity Guide on page 110 for the amount of sugarpaste needed to cover different-sized cakes. The quantities below will give you enough sugarpaste to cover the tops and sides of your cakes.

Sugarpaste
Round/Square Cakes

Round	13cm	15cm	18cm	20cm
	(5in)	(6in)	(7in)	(8in)
Square	10cm	13cm	15cm	18cm
	(4in)	(5in)	(6in)	(7in)
Icing (confectioners')	450g	450g	900g	900g
Sugar	(1lb/3¼ cups)	(1lb/3¼ cups)	(2lb/6½ cups)	(2lb/6½ cups)
Rose water, lemon juice or kirsh (optional)	to taste	to taste	to taste	to taste
Water	5ml	30ml	45ml	60ml
	(1 tsp)	(2 tbsp)	(3 tbsp)	(4 tbsp)
Powdered gelatine	2 tsp	4 tsp	6 tsp	8 tsp
Liquid glucose	5ml	10ml	15ml	20ml
	(1 tsp)	(2 tsp)	(3 tsp)	(4 tsp)

Royal Icing

See the recipe on page 66 for the method. The following quantities will give you enough royal icing to cover the tops and sides of your cakes.

Royal Icing
Round/Square Cakes

Round	13cm	15cm	18cm	20cm
	(5in)	(6in)	(7in)	(8in)
Square	10cm	13cm	15cm	18cm
	(4in)	(5in)	(6in)	(7in)
Egg whites (albumen)	1	2	3	4
Icing (confectioners')	250g	500g	750g	1kg
Sugar	(9oz/1¾ cups)	(1lb 2oz/3¼ cups)	(1lb 10oz/5 cups)	(2lb 4oz/7 cups)
Glycerine	2.5ml	5ml	7.5ml	10ml
(optional)	(½ tsp)	(1 tsp)	(1½ tsp)	(2 tsp)

the essentials

Royal Icing with Albumen Substitute

The quantities below will give you enough egg-free royal icing to cover the tops and sides of your cakes.

Royal Icing with Albumen Substitute
Round/Square Cakes

Round	13cm	15cm	18cm	20cm
	(5in)	(6in)	(7in)	(8in)
Square	10cm	13cm	15cm	18cm
	(4in)	(5in)	(6in)	(7in)
Albumen substitute	7.5g	15g	22g	30g
	(1/4oz/1 tbsp)	(1/2oz/2 tbsp)	(1oz/1/4 cup)	(1 1/4oz/1/4 cup)
Water	37ml	75ml	115ml	150ml
	(3 tbsp)	(5 tbsp)	(8 tbsp)	(5fl oz)
Icing (confectioners')	250g	500g	750g	1kg
Sugar	(9oz/1 3/4 cups)	(1lb 2oz/3 1/4 cups)	(1lb 10oz/5 cups)	(2lb 4oz/7 cups)
Glycerine (optional)	2.5ml	5ml	7.5ml	10ml
	(1/2 tsp)	(1 tsp)	(1 1/2 tsp)	(2 tsp)

METHOD

1. In a mixing bowl, blend the albumen substitute and the water.
2. Once the albumen substitute has dissolved completely, strain the mixture through a very fine sieve (strainer).
3. Add the icing (confectioners') sugar a spoonful at a time until you have achieved the consistency that you want (see Working with Royal Icing, page 66, for more on this).
4. Blend in the glycerine, if used.

Mexican Paste

If you are pressed for time, you can buy ready-made Mexican paste. Preparing your own is not difficult – indeed, the only hitch is that you need to make it 24 hours before use.

The recipe below gives 1 kg (2lb 4 oz) of Mexican paste. If this is more than you need, cut it into small blocks, wrap these in cling film (plastic wrap) and a plastic bag, and put them in the freezer until required.

250g (9oz/1 ¾ cups) icing (confectioners') sugar
15ml (1 tbsp) gum tragacanth or Tylo powder
5ml (1tsp) liquid glucose
30ml (2 tbsp) cold water

METHOD

1. Stir together the icing (confectioners') sugar and gum tragacanth/Tylo powder in a mixing bowl.
2. Make a small well in the centre of the mixture and add the liquid glucose.
3. Add the water 5ml (1 tsp) at a time, all the while mixing by hand or at a slow speed.
4. Continue adding water and stirring until the paste is thoroughly blended.
5. Wrap the mixture in cling film (plastic wrap) and a plastic bag, and leave it in the refrigerator for 24 hours before use.

Index

A

albumen substitute 125
allergies 18–19

B

Baby Booties (pressure
    piping) 73
ball for modelling 84
Ballerina (modelling) 97–99
bark, sugarpaste 82
Beach Balls (modelling) 85
Bird (pressure piping) 74–75
board(s) 10
    to add texture to 52
    to attach ribbon to 49
    to attach twisted edge to
        53–54
    to cover with sugarpaste
        40–41
bows: ribbon 51
    twisted-edge 54–55
bricks, sugarpaste 82–83
bulbs, to pipe 70
bulrushes, sugarpaste 80–81
burning, to prevent 17
bushes, sugarpaste 78, 79
buttercream 18
    to make 26
    quantities for 121
    to use 26–27, 83
buttons 56

C

cake boxes 108
cake spray 17
cake stand 13, 102
cake wire 10, 25–26
    improvised 26
cakes: to cover with marzipan
    30–32
    to cover with sugarpaste
        33–39
    to cut 108
    dairy-free 114, 119
    diabetic 114, 119–120
    egg-free 113, 117
    gluten-, dairy-, egg-free
        118

gluten-free 112, 116
hexagonal 35–36
to level 24
novelty 39, 61, 109, 110,
    115
number 36–39, 109, 110,
    115
oval 35
portions 109
round 35, 109, 110
square 35–36, 109, 110
tiered 102–106
wedding 102–106
see also fruit cakes;
        sponge cakes
Caterpillar (pressure piping)
    75
Cel stick 10, 52, 64, 65, 79,
    90, 91, 92, 93, 98
chocolate chip sponge cake
    116
chocolate cream filling,
    diabetic 120
chocolate sponge cake 116
chocolate topping, dairy-free
    119
Choirboy (modelling) 90–91
cling film 10, 15, 16–17, 56
Clown (modelling) 92–94
cocktail sticks 10, 60, 66
coeliac disease 18
coffee cream filling, diabetic
    120
coffee sponge cake 116
colour wheel 42–43
colours, to mix 42
comic figures 94
cone for modelling 84
confectionery glaze 95
cornflour 91
cream filling, diabetic 120
crimpers/crimping 10,
    57–58
cut-outs 58–59
cutting cakes in half 25–26
cylinder for modelling 84

D

dairy allergy 19

dairy-free chocolate topping
    119
dairy-free fruit cake 114
dairy-free sponge cake 119
decorating bags see piping
    bags
dental floss 26
diabetes 19
diabetic cream filling 120
diabetic fruit cake 114
diabetic sponge cake
    119–120
Dog (modelling) 86–87
Dog (pressure piping) 75–76
dots, to pipe 70
dowels 10, 103–104
Duck (modelling) 85–86

E

E-number allergy 19, 32
edges: sausage 39, 51
    twisted 52–54
egg allergy 18–19
egg-free fruit cake 113
egg-free marzipan 122
egg-free sponge cake 117
Elephant (modelling) 89–90
embossers/embossing 10, 39,
    56–57
equipment 10–13

F

figures, modelled 85
    Ballerina 97–99
    Choirboy 90–91
    Clown 92–94
    comic 94
    to dry 91
    Gentleman 94–96
fir tree, sugarpaste 79
fleurs de lys, to pipe 69
flowerpaste 53
foil, kitchen 10, 56
food allergies 18–19
food colouring 10, 41, 42
    in marzipan 84
    to paint with 61
food dust 10, 81, 82

food intolerances 18, 19
frames (number tins) 14
   to line 16
freezing 18, 22
frills 64–65
fruit cakes: to cover with
   marzipan 30–32
   dairy-free 114
   diabetic 114
   egg-free 113
   to feed 22
   to freeze 22
   gluten-free 112
   to keep moist during
      baking 17
   to make 22–23
   portions 109
   quantities for 111
   to store 18, 22

G

garrett frill cutter 10, 64, 65,
   90–91, 92–93
Gentleman (modelling) 94–96
glacé icing 71
gluten-, dairy-, egg-free
   sponge cake 118
gluten-free fruit cake 112
gluten-free sponge cake 116
gluten intolerance 18
glycerine 66, 76
grass, sugarpaste 78, 79
greaseproof paper 10, 15
gum tragacanth 80, 82, 84

H

hexagonal cakes, to cover
   35–36

I

icing ruler 10, 82–83
inner crimping 58
inserts 59–60

J

jam glaze 30

K

kitchen foil 10, 56
kitchen paper 13, 51

L

lace work 76–77
lemon sponge cake 116
levelling cakes 24
liners, reusable 14
lining 15–16
log, sugarpaste 80

M

marbling: sponge cake 116
   sugarpaste 44–45
marzipan 18, 19
   to cover cakes with 30–32
   egg-free 122
   to make 30
   for modelling 84
   nut-free 123
   quantities for 121
masking tape 55
Mexican paste 60
   to make 125
   for modelling 84
modelling 84–85
   Ballerina 97–99
   Beach Balls 85
   Choirboy 90–91
   Clown 92–94
   comic figures 94
   Dog 86–87
   Duck 85–86
   Elephant 89–90
   Gentleman 94–96
   Teddy Bear 87–88
mortar effect 83
moss effect 82
mouths on models 97
mud, sugarpaste 81

N

novelty cakes: to cover 39
   marzipan for 110
   to paint 61
   portions 109
   quantities 115
   sugarpaste for 110
novelty tins 14–15
   to line 16–17
nozzles see piping tubes
number cakes: to cover
   36–39
   marzipan for 110
   portions 109
   quantities 115

   sugarpaste for 110
number tins see frames
nut allergy 19
nut-free marzipan 123

O

orange sponge cake 116
oval cakes, to cover 35
overlaying 59

P

painting 61
pans see tins
pebbles, sugarpaste 79
pillars 13, 103–106
piping 66–67
   bulbs 70
   dots 70
   fleurs de lys 69
   over embossing 57
   pressure piping 72–
      73
   scrolls 70
   shells 69
   snail trails 69
   stars 71
   straight lines 70–71
   trellises 71
   tube embroidery 72
piping bags 13, 66
   to fill 68
   to make 67
piping gel 78
piping tubes 13, 66, 67
   to insert 68
pizza wheel 13, 37, 60
plastic wrap see cling film
portion guide 109
pressure piping 72–73
   Baby Booties 73
   Bird 74–75
   Caterpillar 75
   Dog 75–76
   Rabbit (Back View) 73
   Teddy Bear 74

Q

quilling 60–61
quilting effect 52

index

R

Rabbit (Back View) (pressure piping) 73
ratios for tiered cakes 102
ready-to-roll icing *see* sugarpaste
ribbons: to attach to boards 49
  to attach to cakes 48–49
rocks, sugarpaste 79
rolled fondant *see* sugarpaste
round cakes: to cover 35
  marzipan for 110
  portions 109
  sugarpaste for 110
royal icing 18, 83
  with albumen substitute 125
  to colour 66–67
  full-peak 66
  lace work 76–77
  to make 66
  to pipe 57, 66–71
  pressure piping 72–76
  quantities for 124
  soft-peak 66
  to stipple 55–56
  tube embroidery 72
  wave crests 79

S

sand effect 81
sausage edges 39, 51
scourer 56, 78
scriber 13, 82
scrolls, to pipe 70
semolina 81
separators 13, 105
shells, to pipe 69
side smoother 13, 35, 36
side templates 64
smoother 13, 34, 37
snail trails, to pipe 69
spaghetti pieces 80, 92, 94
special dietary needs 18–19
  see also dairy-free;
    diabetic; egg-free;
    gluten-free; nut-free
sponge cake: chocolate 116
  chocolate chip 116
  coffee 116
  to cover with marzipan 30
  to cut in half 25–26
  dairy-free 119
  diabetic 119–120

egg-free 117
to extend life of 23
to fill 26–27
to freeze 23
gluten-, dairy, egg-free 118
gluten-free 116
lemon 116
to level 24
to make 23–24
marbled 116
orange 116
portions 109
quantities 115
St Clements 116
to store 23
sponging *see* stippling
square cakes: to cover 35–36
  marzipan for 110
  portions 109
  sugarpaste for 110
St Clements cake 116
stars, to pipe 71
stippling 55–56
stonework, sugarpaste 83
storage 18, 22, 23, 108
straight lines, to pipe 70–71
sugar 81
sugar glue 84
sugarcraft gun 54
sugarpaste 18, 19
  bark 82
  bricks 82–83
  bulrushes 80–81
  bushes 78
  to colour 41–42
  to cover board with 40–41
  to cover cake and board with 33–36
  to cover novelty cakes with 39
  to cover number cakes with 36–39
  cracking 37
  fir tree 79
  to freeze 34
  grass 78
  to knead 33
  log 80
  to make 32–33
  to marble 44–45
  for modelling 84
  mud 81
  pebbles and rocks 79
  purple 45
  quantities for 124

to roll out 33
sand 81
stonework 83

T

Teddy Bear (modelling) 87–88
Teddy Bear (pressure piping) 74
templates, side 64
texture, to add to board 52
tiered cakes 102
  with pillars 103–106
  ratios 102
  stacked 106
  with stand 102
tile spacers 52
till roll 36
tins 13
  to clean 15
  to line 15–16
  novelty 14–15, 16–17
  number (frames) 14, 16
  types 14
tools 10–13
transportation 108
trellises, to pipe 71
tube embroidery 72
twisted edges 52–53
  to attach to board 53–54
  to attach to cake 54
Tylo powder 80, 82, 84

W

wallpaper 52
watermark, to avoid 51
waxed paper *see* greaseproof paper
wedding cake 102
  with pillars 103–106
  ratios 102
  stacked 106
  with stand 102

8/09